Address _____ Price _____

Bedrooms _____ Bathrooms _____ Sq.Ft. _____

Lot Size: _____ Year Built _____ School District _____

Annual Tax _____

EXTERIOR

	Good	Average	Poor
View/Yard/Landscaping	☐	☐	☐
Trees	☐	☐	☐
Lawn (Front)	☐	☐	☐
Lawn (Back)	☐	☐	☐
Fences (condition)	☐	☐	☐
Landscaping (condition)	☐	☐	☐
Irrigation / Sprinkler	☐	☐	☐
	☐	☐	☐
House Type	☐	☐	☐
Exterior Siding	☐	☐	☐
Deck / Patio / Porch	☐	☐	☐
Garage	☐	☐	☐
Window / Doors	☐	☐	☐
Roof / Gutters	☐	☐	☐
Fencing	☐	☐	☐

HOME SYSTEMS

	Good	Average	Poor
Electrical	☐	☐	☐
Air Conditioning / Fans	☐	☐	☐
Heating	☐	☐	☐
Security	☐	☐	☐
Plumbing	☐	☐	☐
Intercom	☐	☐	☐

FEATURES

	Good	Average	Poor
Home Warranty	☐	☐	☐
Energy Saving Features	☐	☐	☐

INTERIOR

	Good	Average	Poor
Walls / Trim / Ceilings	☐	☐	☐
Flooring	☐	☐	☐
Stairs	☐	☐	☐
Storage	☐	☐	☐
Living Room	☐	☐	☐
Family Room	☐	☐	☐
Dining Room	☐	☐	☐

	Good	Average	Poor
Master Bedroom	☐	☐	☐
Bedroom 2	☐	☐	☐
Bedroom 3	☐	☐	☐
Bedroom 4	☐	☐	☐
Master Bathroom	☐	☐	☐
Bathroom 2	☐	☐	☐
Bathroom 3	☐	☐	☐
Bonus / Game Room	☐	☐	☐

	Good	Average	Poor
Kitchen	☐	☐	☐
Cabinets	☐	☐	☐
Countertop	☐	☐	☐
Counter Space	☐	☐	☐
Flooring	☐	☐	☐
Oven / Stove	☐	☐	☐
Microwave	☐	☐	☐
Layout	☐	☐	☐
Light Fixtures	☐	☐	☐
Backsplash	☐	☐	☐
Pantry	☐	☐	☐
Appliances	☐	☐	☐
Island	☐	☐	☐

	Good	Average	Poor
Basement	☐	☐	☐
Garage	☐	☐	☐

COMMUNITY

	Good	Average	Poor
Immediate Neighborhood	☐	☐	☐
Close to Employment	☐	☐	☐
Close to Shopping	☐	☐	☐
Close to Transportation	☐	☐	☐
Close to Schools / Daycare	☐	☐	☐
Close to Places of Worship	☐	☐	☐
Near Recreational Facilities	☐	☐	☐
Close to Airport	☐	☐	☐
Near Police and Fire Department	☐	☐	☐

Address _____ Price _____

Bedrooms _____ Bathrooms _____ Sq.Ft. _____

Lot Size: _____ Year Built _____ School District _____

Annual Tax _____

EXTERIOR

	Good	Average	Poor
View/Yard/Landscaping	☐	☐	☐
Trees	☐	☐	☐
Lawn (Front)	☐	☐	☐
Lawn (Back)	☐	☐	☐
Fences (condition)	☐	☐	☐
Landscaping (condition)	☐	☐	☐
Irrigation / Sprinkler	☐	☐	☐
	☐	☐	☐
House Type	☐	☐	☐
Exterior Siding	☐	☐	☐
Deck / Patio / Porch	☐	☐	☐
Garage	☐	☐	☐
Window / Doors	☐	☐	☐
Roof / Gutters	☐	☐	☐
Fencing	☐	☐	☐

HOME SYSTEMS

	Good	Average	Poor
Electrical	☐	☐	☐
Air Conditioning / Fans	☐	☐	☐
Heating	☐	☐	☐
Security	☐	☐	☐
Plumbing	☐	☐	☐
Intercom	☐	☐	☐

FEATURES

	Good	Average	Poor
Home Warranty	☐	☐	☐
Energy Saving Features	☐	☐	☐

INTERIOR

	Good	Average	Poor
Walls / Trim / Ceilings	☐	☐	☐
Flooring	☐	☐	☐
Stairs	☐	☐	☐
Storage	☐	☐	☐
Living Room	☐	☐	☐
Family Room	☐	☐	☐
Dining Room	☐	☐	☐

	Good	Average	Poor
Master Bedroom	☐	☐	☐
Bedroom 2	☐	☐	☐
Bedroom 3	☐	☐	☐
Bedroom 4	☐	☐	☐
Master Bathroom	☐	☐	☐
Bathroom 2	☐	☐	☐
Bathroom 3	☐	☐	☐
Bonus / Game Room	☐	☐	☐

	Good	Average	Poor
Kitchen	☐	☐	☐
Cabinets	☐	☐	☐
Countertop	☐	☐	☐
Counter Space	☐	☐	☐
Flooring	☐	☐	☐
Oven / Stove	☐	☐	☐
Microwave	☐	☐	☐
Layout	☐	☐	☐
Light Fixtures	☐	☐	☐
Backsplash	☐	☐	☐
Pantry	☐	☐	☐
Appliances	☐	☐	☐
Island	☐	☐	☐

	Good	Average	Poor
Basement	☐	☐	☐
Garage	☐	☐	☐

COMMUNITY

	Good	Average	Poor
Immediate Neighborhood	☐	☐	☐
Close to Employment	☐	☐	☐
Close to Shopping	☐	☐	☐
Close to Transportation	☐	☐	☐
Close to Schools / Daycare	☐	☐	☐
Close to Places of Worship	☐	☐	☐
Near Recreational Facilities	☐	☐	☐
Close to Airport	☐	☐	☐
Near Police and Fire Department	☐	☐	☐

Address _____ Price _____

Bedrooms _____ Bathrooms _____ Sq.Ft. _____

Lot Size: _____ Year Built _____ School District _____

Annual Tax _____

EXTERIOR

	Good	Average	Poor
View/Yard/Landscaping	☐	☐	☐
Trees	☐	☐	☐
Lawn (Front)	☐	☐	☐
Lawn (Back)	☐	☐	☐
Fences (condition)	☐	☐	☐
Landscaping (condition)	☐	☐	☐
Irrigation / Sprinkler	☐	☐	☐
	☐	☐	☐
House Type	☐	☐	☐
Exterior Siding	☐	☐	☐
Deck / Patio / Porch	☐	☐	☐
Garage	☐	☐	☐
Window / Doors	☐	☐	☐
Roof / Gutters	☐	☐	☐
Fencing	☐	☐	☐

HOME SYSTEMS

	Good	Average	Poor
Electrical	☐	☐	☐
Air Conditioning / Fans	☐	☐	☐
Heating	☐	☐	☐
Security	☐	☐	☐
Plumbing	☐	☐	☐
Intercom	☐	☐	☐

FEATURES

	Good	Average	Poor
Home Warranty	☐	☐	☐
Energy Saving Features	☐	☐	☐

INTERIOR

	Good	Average	Poor
Walls / Trim / Ceilings	☐	☐	☐
Flooring	☐	☐	☐
Stairs	☐	☐	☐
Storage	☐	☐	☐
Living Room	☐	☐	☐
Family Room	☐	☐	☐
Dining Room	☐	☐	☐

	Good	Average	Poor
Master Bedroom	☐	☐	☐
Bedroom 2	☐	☐	☐
Bedroom 3	☐	☐	☐
Bedroom 4	☐	☐	☐
Master Bathroom	☐	☐	☐
Bathroom 2	☐	☐	☐
Bathroom 3	☐	☐	☐
Bonus / Game Room	☐	☐	☐

	Good	Average	Poor
Kitchen			
Cabinets	☐	☐	☐
Countertop	☐	☐	☐
Counter Space	☐	☐	☐
Flooring	☐	☐	☐
Oven / Stove	☐	☐	☐
Microwave	☐	☐	☐
Layout	☐	☐	☐
Light Fixtures	☐	☐	☐
Backsplash	☐	☐	☐
Pantry	☐	☐	☐
Appliances	☐	☐	☐
Island	☐	☐	☐

	Good	Average	Poor
Basement	☐	☐	☐
Garage	☐	☐	☐

COMMUNITY

	Good	Average	Poor
Immediate Neighborhood	☐	☐	☐
Close to Employment	☐	☐	☐
Close to Shopping	☐	☐	☐
Close to Transportation	☐	☐	☐
Close to Schools / Daycare	☐	☐	☐
Close to Places of Worship	☐	☐	☐
Near Recreational Facilities	☐	☐	☐
Close to Airport	☐	☐	☐
Near Police and Fire Department	☐	☐	☐

Address _____ Price _____

Bedrooms _____ Bathrooms _____ Sq.Ft. _____

Lot Size: _____ Year Built _____ School District _____

Annual Tax _____

EXTERIOR

	Good	Average	Poor
View/Yard/Landscaping	☐	☐	☐
Trees	☐	☐	☐
Lawn (Front)	☐	☐	☐
Lawn (Back)	☐	☐	☐
Fences (condition)	☐	☐	☐
Landscaping (condition)	☐	☐	☐
Irrigation / Sprinkler	☐	☐	☐
	☐	☐	☐
House Type	☐	☐	☐
Exterior Siding	☐	☐	☐
Deck / Patio / Porch	☐	☐	☐
Garage	☐	☐	☐
Window / Doors	☐	☐	☐
Roof / Gutters	☐	☐	☐
Fencing	☐	☐	☐

HOME SYSTEMS

	Good	Average	Poor
Electrical	☐	☐	☐
Air Conditioning / Fans	☐	☐	☐
Heating	☐	☐	☐
Security	☐	☐	☐
Plumbing	☐	☐	☐
Intercom	☐	☐	☐

FEATURES

	Good	Average	Poor
Home Warranty	☐	☐	☐
Energy Saving Features	☐	☐	☐

INTERIOR

	Good	Average	Poor
Walls / Trim / Ceilings	☐	☐	☐
Flooring	☐	☐	☐
Stairs	☐	☐	☐
Storage	☐	☐	☐
Living Room	☐	☐	☐
Family Room	☐	☐	☐
Dining Room	☐	☐	☐

	Good	Average	Poor
Master Bedroom	☐	☐	☐
Bedroom 2	☐	☐	☐
Bedroom 3	☐	☐	☐
Bedroom 4	☐	☐	☐
Master Bathroom	☐	☐	☐
Bathroom 2	☐	☐	☐
Bathroom 3	☐	☐	☐
Bonus / Game Room	☐	☐	☐

	Good	Average	Poor
Kitchen	☐	☐	☐
Cabinets	☐	☐	☐
Countertop	☐	☐	☐
Counter Space	☐	☐	☐
Flooring	☐	☐	☐
Oven / Stove	☐	☐	☐
Microwave	☐	☐	☐
Layout	☐	☐	☐
Light Fixtures	☐	☐	☐
Backsplash	☐	☐	☐
Pantry	☐	☐	☐
Appliances	☐	☐	☐
Island	☐	☐	☐

	Good	Average	Poor
Basement	☐	☐	☐
Garage	☐	☐	☐

COMMUNITY

	Good	Average	Poor
Immediate Neighborhood	☐	☐	☐
Close to Employment	☐	☐	☐
Close to Shopping	☐	☐	☐
Close to Transportation	☐	☐	☐
Close to Schools / Daycare	☐	☐	☐
Close to Places of Worship	☐	☐	☐
Near Recreational Facilities	☐	☐	☐
Close to Airport	☐	☐	☐
Near Police and Fire Department	☐	☐	☐

Address _____   Price _____

Bedrooms _____   Bathrooms _____   Sq.Ft. _____

Lot Size: _____   Year Built _____   School District _____

Annual Tax _____

EXTERIOR

	Good	Average	Poor
View/Yard/Landscaping	☐	☐	☐
Trees	☐	☐	☐
Lawn (Front)	☐	☐	☐
Lawn (Back)	☐	☐	☐
Fences (condition)	☐	☐	☐
Landscaping (condition)	☐	☐	☐
Irrigation / Sprinkler	☐	☐	☐
House Type	☐	☐	☐
Exterior Siding	☐	☐	☐
Deck / Patio / Porch	☐	☐	☐
Garage	☐	☐	☐
Window / Doors	☐	☐	☐
Roof / Gutters	☐	☐	☐
Fencing	☐	☐	☐

HOME SYSTEMS

	Good	Average	Poor
Electrical	☐	☐	☐
Air Conditioning / Fans	☐	☐	☐
Heating	☐	☐	☐
Security	☐	☐	☐
Plumbing	☐	☐	☐
Intercom	☐	☐	☐

FEATURES

	Good	Average	Poor
Home Warranty	☐	☐	☐
Energy Saving Features	☐	☐	☐

INTERIOR

	Good	Average	Poor
Walls / Trim / Ceilings	☐	☐	☐
Flooring	☐	☐	☐
Stairs	☐	☐	☐
Storage	☐	☐	☐
Living Room	☐	☐	☐
Family Room	☐	☐	☐
Dining Room	☐	☐	☐

	Good	Average	Poor
Master Bedroom	☐	☐	☐
Bedroom 2	☐	☐	☐
Bedroom 3	☐	☐	☐
Bedroom 4	☐	☐	☐
Master Bathroom	☐	☐	☐
Bathroom 2	☐	☐	☐
Bathroom 3	☐	☐	☐
Bonus / Game Room	☐	☐	☐

	Good	Average	Poor
Kitchen	☐	☐	☐
Cabinets	☐	☐	☐
Countertop	☐	☐	☐
Counter Space	☐	☐	☐
Flooring	☐	☐	☐
Oven / Stove	☐	☐	☐
Microwave	☐	☐	☐
Layout	☐	☐	☐
Light Fixtures	☐	☐	☐
Backsplash	☐	☐	☐
Pantry	☐	☐	☐
Appliances	☐	☐	☐
Island	☐	☐	☐

	Good	Average	Poor
Basement	☐	☐	☐
Garage	☐	☐	☐

COMMUNITY

	Good	Average	Poor
Immediate Neighborhood	☐	☐	☐
Close to Employment	☐	☐	☐
Close to Shopping	☐	☐	☐
Close to Transportation	☐	☐	☐
Close to Schools / Daycare	☐	☐	☐
Close to Places of Worship	☐	☐	☐
Near Recreational Facilities	☐	☐	☐
Close to Airport	☐	☐	☐
Near Police and Fire Department	☐	☐	☐

Address _____   Price _____

Bedrooms _____ Bathrooms _____ Sq.Ft. _____

Lot Size: _____ Year Built _____ School District _____

Annual Tax _____

EXTERIOR

	Good	Average	Poor
View/Yard/Landscaping	☐	☐	☐
Trees	☐	☐	☐
Lawn (Front)	☐	☐	☐
Lawn (Back)	☐	☐	☐
Fences (condition)	☐	☐	☐
Landscaping (condition)	☐	☐	☐
Irrigation / Sprinkler	☐	☐	☐
	☐	☐	☐
House Type	☐	☐	☐
Exterior Siding	☐	☐	☐
Deck / Patio / Porch	☐	☐	☐
Garage	☐	☐	☐
Window / Doors	☐	☐	☐
Roof / Gutters	☐	☐	☐
Fencing	☐	☐	☐

HOME SYSTEMS

	Good	Average	Poor
Electrical	☐	☐	☐
Air Conditioning / Fans	☐	☐	☐
Heating	☐	☐	☐
Security	☐	☐	☐
Plumbing	☐	☐	☐
Intercom	☐	☐	☐

FEATURES

	Good	Average	Poor
Home Warranty	☐	☐	☐
Energy Saving Features	☐	☐	☐

INTERIOR

	Good	Average	Poor
Walls / Trim / Ceilings	☐	☐	☐
Flooring	☐	☐	☐
Stairs	☐	☐	☐
Storage	☐	☐	☐
Living Room	☐	☐	☐
Family Room	☐	☐	☐
Dining Room	☐	☐	☐

	Good	Average	Poor
Master Bedroom	☐	☐	☐
Bedroom 2	☐	☐	☐
Bedroom 3	☐	☐	☐
Bedroom 4	☐	☐	☐
Master Bathroom	☐	☐	☐
Bathroom 2	☐	☐	☐
Bathroom 3	☐	☐	☐
Bonus / Game Room	☐	☐	☐

	Good	Average	Poor
Kitchen	☐	☐	
Cabinets	☐	☐	☐
Countertop	☐	☐	☐
Counter Space	☐	☐	☐
Flooring	☐	☐	☐
Oven / Stove	☐	☐	☐
Microwave	☐	☐	☐
Layout	☐	☐	☐
Light Fixtures	☐	☐	☐
Backsplash	☐	☐	☐
Pantry	☐	☐	☐
Appliances	☐	☐	☐
Island	☐	☐	☐

	Good	Average	Poor
Basement	☐	☐	☐
Garage	☐	☐	☐

COMMUNITY

	Good	Average	Poor
Immediate Neighborhood	☐	☐	☐
Close to Employment	☐	☐	☐
Close to Shopping	☐	☐	☐
Close to Transportation	☐	☐	☐
Close to Schools / Daycare	☐	☐	☐
Close to Places of Worship	☐	☐	☐
Near Recreational Facilities	☐	☐	☐
Close to Airport	☐	☐	☐
Near Police and Fire Department	☐	☐	☐

Address _____ Price _____

Bedrooms _____ Bathrooms _____ Sq.Ft. _____

Lot Size: _____ Year Built _____ School District _____

Annual Tax _____

EXTERIOR

	Good	Average	Poor
View/Yard/Landscaping	☐	☐	☐
Trees	☐	☐	☐
Lawn (Front)	☐	☐	☐
Lawn (Back)	☐	☐	☐
Fences (condition)	☐	☐	☐
Landscaping (condition)	☐	☐	☐
Irrigation / Sprinkler	☐	☐	☐
	☐	☐	☐
House Type	☐	☐	☐
Exterior Siding	☐	☐	☐
Deck / Patio / Porch	☐	☐	☐
Garage	☐	☐	☐
Window / Doors	☐	☐	☐
Roof / Gutters	☐	☐	☐
Fencing	☐	☐	☐

HOME SYSTEMS

	Good	Average	Poor
Electrical	☐	☐	☐
Air Conditioning / Fans	☐	☐	☐
Heating	☐	☐	☐
Security	☐	☐	☐
Plumbing	☐	☐	☐
Intercom	☐	☐	☐

FEATURES

	Good	Average	Poor
Home Warranty	☐	☐	☐
Energy Saving Features	☐	☐	☐

INTERIOR

	Good	Average	Poor
Walls / Trim / Ceilings	☐	☐	☐
Flooring	☐	☐	☐
Stairs	☐	☐	☐
Storage	☐	☐	☐
Living Room	☐	☐	☐
Family Room	☐	☐	☐
Dining Room	☐	☐	☐

	Good	Average	Poor
Master Bedroom	☐	☐	☐
Bedroom 2	☐	☐	☐
Bedroom 3	☐	☐	☐
Bedroom 4	☐	☐	☐
Master Bathroom	☐	☐	☐
Bathroom 2	☐	☐	☐
Bathroom 3	☐	☐	☐
Bonus / Game Room	☐	☐	☐

	Good	Average	Poor
Kitchen			
Cabinets	☐	☐	☐
Countertop	☐	☐	☐
Counter Space	☐	☐	☐
Flooring	☐	☐	☐
Oven / Stove	☐	☐	☐
Microwave	☐	☐	☐
Layout	☐	☐	☐
Light Fixtures	☐	☐	☐
Backsplash	☐	☐	☐
Pantry	☐	☐	☐
Appliances	☐	☐	☐
Island	☐	☐	☐

	Good	Average	Poor
Basement	☐	☐	☐
Garage	☐	☐	☐

COMMUNITY

	Good	Average	Poor
Immediate Neighborhood	☐	☐	☐
Close to Employment	☐	☐	☐
Close to Shopping	☐	☐	☐
Close to Transportation	☐	☐	☐
Close to Schools / Daycare	☐	☐	☐
Close to Places of Worship	☐	☐	☐
Near Recreational Facilities	☐	☐	☐
Close to Airport	☐	☐	☐
Near Police and Fire Department	☐	☐	☐

Address _____ Price _____

Bedrooms _____ Bathrooms _____ Sq.Ft. _____

Lot Size: _____ Year Built _____ School District _____

Annual Tax _____

EXTERIOR

	Good	Average	Poor
View/Yard/Landscaping	☐	☐	☐
Trees	☐	☐	☐
Lawn (Front)	☐	☐	☐
Lawn (Back)	☐	☐	☐
Fences (condition)	☐	☐	☐
Landscaping (condition)	☐	☐	☐
Irrigation / Sprinkler	☐	☐	☐
	☐	☐	☐
House Type	☐	☐	☐
Exterior Siding	☐	☐	☐
Deck / Patio / Porch	☐	☐	☐
Garage	☐	☐	☐
Window / Doors	☐	☐	☐
Roof / Gutters	☐	☐	☐
Fencing	☐	☐	☐

HOME SYSTEMS

	Good	Average	Poor
Electrical	☐	☐	☐
Air Conditioning / Fans	☐	☐	☐
Heating	☐	☐	☐
Security	☐	☐	☐
Plumbing	☐	☐	☐
Intercom	☐	☐	☐

FEATURES

	Good	Average	Poor
Home Warranty	☐	☐	☐
Energy Saving Features	☐	☐	☐

INTERIOR

	Good	Average	Poor
Walls / Trim / Ceilings	☐	☐	☐
Flooring	☐	☐	☐
Stairs	☐	☐	☐
Storage	☐	☐	☐
Living Room	☐	☐	☐
Family Room	☐	☐	☐
Dining Room	☐	☐	☐

	Good	Average	Poor
Master Bedroom	☐	☐	☐
Bedroom 2	☐	☐	☐
Bedroom 3	☐	☐	☐
Bedroom 4	☐	☐	☐
Master Bathroom	☐	☐	☐
Bathroom 2	☐	☐	☐
Bathroom 3	☐	☐	☐
Bonus / Game Room	☐	☐	☐

	Good	Average	Poor
Kitchen			
Cabinets	☐	☐	☐
Countertop	☐	☐	☐
Counter Space	☐	☐	☐
Flooring	☐	☐	☐
Oven / Stove	☐	☐	☐
Microwave	☐	☐	☐
Layout	☐	☐	☐
Light Fixtures	☐	☐	☐
Backsplash	☐	☐	☐
Pantry	☐	☐	☐
Appliances	☐	☐	☐
Island	☐	☐	☐

	Good	Average	Poor
Basement	☐	☐	☐
Garage	☐	☐	☐

COMMUNITY

	Good	Average	Poor
Immediate Neighborhood	☐	☐	☐
Close to Employment	☐	☐	☐
Close to Shopping	☐	☐	☐
Close to Transportation	☐	☐	☐
Close to Schools / Daycare	☐	☐	☐
Close to Places of Worship	☐	☐	☐
Near Recreational Facilities	☐	☐	☐
Close to Airport	☐	☐	☐
Near Police and Fire Department	☐	☐	☐

Address _____ Price _____

Bedrooms _____ Bathrooms _____ Sq.Ft. _____

Lot Size: _____ Year Built _____ School District _____

Annual Tax _____

EXTERIOR

	Good	Average	Poor
View/Yard/Landscaping	☐	☐	☐
Trees	☐	☐	☐
Lawn (Front)	☐	☐	☐
Lawn (Back)	☐	☐	☐
Fences (condition)	☐	☐	☐
Landscaping (condition)	☐	☐	☐
Irrigation / Sprinkler	☐	☐	☐
House Type	☐	☐	☐
Exterior Siding	☐	☐	☐
Deck / Patio / Porch	☐	☐	☐
Garage	☐	☐	☐
Window / Doors	☐	☐	☐
Roof / Gutters	☐	☐	☐
Fencing	☐	☐	☐

HOME SYSTEMS

	Good	Average	Poor
Electrical	☐	☐	☐
Air Conditioning / Fans	☐	☐	☐
Heating	☐	☐	☐
Security	☐	☐	☐
Plumbing	☐	☐	☐
Intercom	☐	☐	☐

FEATURES

	Good	Average	Poor
Home Warranty	☐	☐	☐
Energy Saving Features	☐	☐	☐

INTERIOR

	Good	Average	Poor
Walls / Trim / Ceilings	☐	☐	☐
Flooring	☐	☐	☐
Stairs	☐	☐	☐
Storage	☐	☐	☐
Living Room	☐	☐	☐
Family Room	☐	☐	☐
Dining Room	☐	☐	☐

	Good	Average	Poor
Master Bedroom	☐	☐	☐
Bedroom 2	☐	☐	☐
Bedroom 3	☐	☐	☐
Bedroom 4	☐	☐	☐
Master Bathroom	☐	☐	☐
Bathroom 2	☐	☐	☐
Bathroom 3	☐	☐	☐
Bonus / Game Room	☐	☐	☐

	Good	Average	Poor
Kitchen	☐	☐	☐
Cabinets	☐	☐	☐
Countertop	☐	☐	☐
Counter Space	☐	☐	☐
Flooring	☐	☐	☐
Oven / Stove	☐	☐	☐
Microwave	☐	☐	☐
Layout	☐	☐	☐
Light Fixtures	☐	☐	☐
Backsplash	☐	☐	☐
Pantry	☐	☐	☐
Appliances	☐	☐	☐
Island	☐	☐	☐

	Good	Average	Poor
Basement	☐	☐	☐
Garage	☐	☐	☐

COMMUNITY

	Good	Average	Poor
Immediate Neighborhood	☐	☐	☐
Close to Employment	☐	☐	☐
Close to Shopping	☐	☐	☐
Close to Transportation	☐	☐	☐
Close to Schools / Daycare	☐	☐	☐
Close to Places of Worship	☐	☐	☐
Near Recreational Facilities	☐	☐	☐
Close to Airport	☐	☐	☐
Near Police and Fire Department	☐	☐	☐

Address _____ Price _____

Bedrooms _____ Bathrooms _____ Sq.Ft. _____

Lot Size: _____ Year Built _____ School District _____

Annual Tax _____

EXTERIOR

	Good	Average	Poor
View/Yard/Landscaping	☐	☐	☐
Trees	☐	☐	☐
Lawn (Front)	☐	☐	☐
Lawn (Back)	☐	☐	☐
Fences (condition)	☐	☐	☐
Landscaping (condition)	☐	☐	☐
Irrigation / Sprinkler	☐	☐	☐
	☐	☐	☐
House Type	☐	☐	☐
Exterior Siding	☐	☐	☐
Deck / Patio / Porch	☐	☐	☐
Garage	☐	☐	☐
Window / Doors	☐	☐	☐
Roof / Gutters	☐	☐	☐
Fencing	☐	☐	☐

HOME SYSTEMS

	Good	Average	Poor
Electrical	☐	☐	☐
Air Conditioning / Fans	☐	☐	☐
Heating	☐	☐	☐
Security	☐	☐	☐
Plumbing	☐	☐	☐
Intercom	☐	☐	☐

FEATURES

	Good	Average	Poor
Home Warranty	☐	☐	☐
Energy Saving Features	☐	☐	☐

INTERIOR

	Good	Average	Poor
Walls / Trim / Ceilings	☐	☐	☐
Flooring	☐	☐	☐
Stairs	☐	☐	☐
Storage	☐	☐	☐
Living Room	☐	☐	☐
Family Room	☐	☐	☐
Dining Room	☐	☐	☐

	Good	Average	Poor
Master Bedroom	☐	☐	☐
Bedroom 2	☐	☐	☐
Bedroom 3	☐	☐	☐
Bedroom 4	☐	☐	☐
Master Bathroom	☐	☐	☐
Bathroom 2	☐	☐	☐
Bathroom 3	☐	☐	☐
Bonus / Game Room	☐	☐	☐

	Good	Average	Poor
Kitchen	☐	☐	☐
Cabinets	☐	☐	☐
Countertop	☐	☐	☐
Counter Space	☐	☐	☐
Flooring	☐	☐	☐
Oven / Stove	☐	☐	☐
Microwave	☐	☐	☐
Layout	☐	☐	☐
Light Fixtures	☐	☐	☐
Backsplash	☐	☐	☐
Pantry	☐	☐	☐
Appliances	☐	☐	☐
Island	☐	☐	☐

	Good	Average	Poor
Basement	☐	☐	☐
Garage	☐	☐	☐

COMMUNITY

	Good	Average	Poor
Immediate Neighborhood	☐	☐	☐
Close to Employment	☐	☐	☐
Close to Shopping	☐	☐	☐
Close to Transportation	☐	☐	☐
Close to Schools / Daycare	☐	☐	☐
Close to Places of Worship	☐	☐	☐
Near Recreational Facilities	☐	☐	☐
Close to Airport	☐	☐	☐
Near Police and Fire Department	☐	☐	☐

Address _____ Price _____

Bedrooms _____ Bathrooms _____ Sq.Ft. _____

Lot Size: _____ Year Built _____ School District _____

Annual Tax _____

EXTERIOR

	Good	Average	Poor
View/Yard/Landscaping	☐	☐	☐
Trees	☐	☐	☐
Lawn (Front)	☐	☐	☐
Lawn (Back)	☐	☐	☐
Fences (condition)	☐	☐	☐
Landscaping (condition)	☐	☐	☐
Irrigation / Sprinkler	☐	☐	☐
House Type	☐	☐	☐
Exterior Siding	☐	☐	☐
Deck / Patio / Porch	☐	☐	☐
Garage	☐	☐	☐
Window / Doors	☐	☐	☐
Roof / Gutters	☐	☐	☐
Fencing	☐	☐	☐

HOME SYSTEMS

	Good	Average	Poor
Electrical	☐	☐	☐
Air Conditioning / Fans	☐	☐	☐
Heating	☐	☐	☐
Security	☐	☐	☐
Plumbing	☐	☐	☐
Intercom	☐	☐	☐

FEATURES

	Good	Average	Poor
Home Warranty	☐	☐	☐
Energy Saving Features	☐	☐	☐

INTERIOR

	Good	Average	Poor
Walls / Trim / Ceilings	☐	☐	☐
Flooring	☐	☐	☐
Stairs	☐	☐	☐
Storage	☐	☐	☐
Living Room	☐	☐	☐
Family Room	☐	☐	☐
Dining Room	☐	☐	☐

	Good	Average	Poor
Master Bedroom	☐	☐	☐
Bedroom 2	☐	☐	☐
Bedroom 3	☐	☐	☐
Bedroom 4	☐	☐	☐
Master Bathroom	☐	☐	☐
Bathroom 2	☐	☐	☐
Bathroom 3	☐	☐	☐
Bonus / Game Room	☐	☐	☐

	Good	Average	Poor
Kitchen			
Cabinets	☐	☐	☐
Countertop	☐	☐	☐
Counter Space	☐	☐	☐
Flooring	☐	☐	☐
Oven / Stove	☐	☐	☐
Microwave	☐	☐	☐
Layout	☐	☐	☐
Light Fixtures	☐	☐	☐
Backsplash	☐	☐	☐
Pantry	☐	☐	☐
Appliances	☐	☐	☐
Island	☐	☐	☐

	Good	Average	Poor
Basement	☐	☐	☐
Garage	☐	☐	☐

COMMUNITY

	Good	Average	Poor
Immediate Neighborhood	☐	☐	☐
Close to Employment	☐	☐	☐
Close to Shopping	☐	☐	☐
Close to Transportation	☐	☐	☐
Close to Schools / Daycare	☐	☐	☐
Close to Places of Worship	☐	☐	☐
Near Recreational Facilities	☐	☐	☐
Close to Airport	☐	☐	☐
Near Police and Fire Department	☐	☐	☐

Address _____ Price _____

Bedrooms _____ Bathrooms _____ Sq.Ft. _____

Lot Size: _____ Year Built _____ School District _____

Annual Tax _____

EXTERIOR

	Good	Average	Poor
View/Yard/Landscaping	☐	☐	☐
Trees	☐	☐	☐
Lawn (Front)	☐	☐	☐
Lawn (Back)	☐	☐	☐
Fences (condition)	☐	☐	☐
Landscaping (condition)	☐	☐	☐
Irrigation / Sprinkler	☐	☐	☐
	☐	☐	☐
House Type	☐	☐	☐
Exterior Siding	☐	☐	☐
Deck / Patio / Porch	☐	☐	☐
Garage	☐	☐	☐
Window / Doors	☐	☐	☐
Roof / Gutters	☐	☐	☐
Fencing	☐	☐	☐

HOME SYSTEMS

	Good	Average	Poor
Electrical	☐	☐	☐
Air Conditioning / Fans	☐	☐	☐
Heating	☐	☐	☐
Security	☐	☐	☐
Plumbing	☐	☐	☐
Intercom	☐	☐	☐

FEATURES

	Good	Average	Poor
Home Warranty	☐	☐	☐
Energy Saving Features	☐	☐	☐

INTERIOR

	Good	Average	Poor
Walls / Trim / Ceilings	☐	☐	☐
Flooring	☐	☐	☐
Stairs	☐	☐	☐
Storage	☐	☐	☐
Living Room	☐	☐	☐
Family Room	☐	☐	☐
Dining Room	☐	☐	☐

	Good	Average	Poor
Master Bedroom	☐	☐	☐
Bedroom 2	☐	☐	☐
Bedroom 3	☐	☐	☐
Bedroom 4	☐	☐	☐
Master Bathroom	☐	☐	☐
Bathroom 2	☐	☐	☐
Bathroom 3	☐	☐	☐
Bonus / Game Room	☐	☐	☐

	Good	Average	Poor
Kitchen			
Cabinets	☐	☐	☐
Countertop	☐	☐	☐
Counter Space	☐	☐	☐
Flooring	☐	☐	☐
Oven / Stove	☐	☐	☐
Microwave	☐	☐	☐
Layout	☐	☐	☐
Light Fixtures	☐	☐	☐
Backsplash	☐	☐	☐
Pantry	☐	☐	☐
Appliances	☐	☐	☐
Island	☐	☐	☐

	Good	Average	Poor
Basement	☐	☐	☐
Garage	☐	☐	☐

COMMUNITY

	Good	Average	Poor
Immediate Neighborhood	☐	☐	☐
Close to Employment	☐	☐	☐
Close to Shopping	☐	☐	☐
Close to Transportation	☐	☐	☐
Close to Schools / Daycare	☐	☐	☐
Close to Places of Worship	☐	☐	☐
Near Recreational Facilities	☐	☐	☐
Close to Airport	☐	☐	☐
Near Police and Fire Department	☐	☐	☐

Address _____ Price _____

Bedrooms _____ Bathrooms _____ Sq.Ft. _____

Lot Size: _____ Year Built _____ School District _____

Annual Tax _____

EXTERIOR

	Good	Average	Poor
View/Yard/Landscaping	☐	☐	☐
Trees	☐	☐	☐
Lawn (Front)	☐	☐	☐
Lawn (Back)	☐	☐	☐
Fences (condition)	☐	☐	☐
Landscaping (condition)	☐	☐	☐
Irrigation / Sprinkler	☐	☐	☐
	☐	☐	☐
House Type	☐	☐	☐
Exterior Siding	☐	☐	☐
Deck / Patio / Porch	☐	☐	☐
Garage	☐	☐	☐
Window / Doors	☐	☐	☐
Roof / Gutters	☐	☐	☐
Fencing	☐	☐	☐

HOME SYSTEMS

	Good	Average	Poor
Electrical	☐	☐	☐
Air Conditioning / Fans	☐	☐	☐
Heating	☐	☐	☐
Security	☐	☐	☐
Plumbing	☐	☐	☐
Intercom	☐	☐	☐

FEATURES

	Good	Average	Poor
Home Warranty	☐	☐	☐
Energy Saving Features	☐	☐	☐

INTERIOR

	Good	Average	Poor
Walls / Trim / Ceilings	☐	☐	☐
Flooring	☐	☐	☐
Stairs	☐	☐	☐
Storage	☐	☐	☐
Living Room	☐	☐	☐
Family Room	☐	☐	☐
Dining Room	☐	☐	☐

	Good	Average	Poor
Master Bedroom	☐	☐	☐
Bedroom 2	☐	☐	☐
Bedroom 3	☐	☐	☐
Bedroom 4	☐	☐	☐
Master Bathroom	☐	☐	☐
Bathroom 2	☐	☐	☐
Bathroom 3	☐	☐	☐
Bonus / Game Room	☐	☐	☐

	Good	Average	Poor
Kitchen	☐	☐	☐
Cabinets	☐	☐	☐
Countertop	☐	☐	☐
Counter Space	☐	☐	☐
Flooring	☐	☐	☐
Oven / Stove	☐	☐	☐
Microwave	☐	☐	☐
Layout	☐	☐	☐
Light Fixtures	☐	☐	☐
Backsplash	☐	☐	☐
Pantry	☐	☐	☐
Appliances	☐	☐	☐
Island	☐	☐	☐

	Good	Average	Poor
Basement	☐	☐	☐
Garage	☐	☐	☐

COMMUNITY

	Good	Average	Poor
Immediate Neighborhood	☐	☐	☐
Close to Employment	☐	☐	☐
Close to Shopping	☐	☐	☐
Close to Transportation	☐	☐	☐
Close to Schools / Daycare	☐	☐	☐
Close to Places of Worship	☐	☐	☐
Near Recreational Facilities	☐	☐	☐
Close to Airport	☐	☐	☐
Near Police and Fire Department	☐	☐	☐

Address _____ Price _____

Bedrooms _____ Bathrooms _____ Sq.Ft. _____

Lot Size: _____ Year Built _____ School District _____

Annual Tax _____

EXTERIOR

	Good	Average	Poor
View/Yard/Landscaping	☐	☐	☐
Trees	☐	☐	☐
Lawn (Front)	☐	☐	☐
Lawn (Back)	☐	☐	☐
Fences (condition)	☐	☐	☐
Landscaping (condition)	☐	☐	☐
Irrigation / Sprinkler	☐	☐	☐
	☐	☐	☐
House Type	☐	☐	☐
Exterior Siding	☐	☐	☐
Deck / Patio / Porch	☐	☐	☐
Garage	☐	☐	☐
Window / Doors	☐	☐	☐
Roof / Gutters	☐	☐	☐
Fencing	☐	☐	☐

HOME SYSTEMS

	Good	Average	Poor
Electrical	☐	☐	☐
Air Conditioning / Fans	☐	☐	☐
Heating	☐	☐	☐
Security	☐	☐	☐
Plumbing	☐	☐	☐
Intercom	☐	☐	☐

FEATURES

	Good	Average	Poor
Home Warranty	☐	☐	☐
Energy Saving Features	☐	☐	☐

INTERIOR

	Good	Average	Poor
Walls / Trim / Ceilings	☐	☐	☐
Flooring	☐	☐	☐
Stairs	☐	☐	☐
Storage	☐	☐	☐
Living Room	☐	☐	☐
Family Room	☐	☐	☐
Dining Room	☐	☐	☐

	Good	Average	Poor
Master Bedroom	☐	☐	☐
Bedroom 2	☐	☐	☐
Bedroom 3	☐	☐	☐
Bedroom 4	☐	☐	☐
Master Bathroom	☐	☐	☐
Bathroom 2	☐	☐	☐
Bathroom 3	☐	☐	☐
Bonus / Game Room	☐	☐	☐

	Good	Average	Poor
Kitchen			
Cabinets	☐	☐	☐
Countertop	☐	☐	☐
Counter Space	☐	☐	☐
Flooring	☐	☐	☐
Oven / Stove	☐	☐	☐
Microwave	☐	☐	☐
Layout	☐	☐	☐
Light Fixtures	☐	☐	☐
Backsplash	☐	☐	☐
Pantry	☐	☐	☐
Appliances	☐	☐	☐
Island	☐	☐	☐

	Good	Average	Poor
Basement	☐	☐	☐
Garage	☐	☐	☐

COMMUNITY

	Good	Average	Poor
Immediate Neighborhood	☐	☐	☐
Close to Employment	☐	☐	☐
Close to Shopping	☐	☐	☐
Close to Transportation	☐	☐	☐
Close to Schools / Daycare	☐	☐	☐
Close to Places of Worship	☐	☐	☐
Near Recreational Facilities	☐	☐	☐
Close to Airport	☐	☐	☐
Near Police and Fire Department	☐	☐	☐

Address _____ Price _____

Bedrooms _____ Bathrooms _____ Sq.Ft. _____

Lot Size: _____ Year Built _____ School District _____

Annual Tax _____

EXTERIOR

	Good	Average	Poor
View/Yard/Landscaping	☐	☐	☐
Trees	☐	☐	☐
Lawn (Front)	☐	☐	☐
Lawn (Back)	☐	☐	☐
Fences (condition)	☐	☐	☐
Landscaping (condition)	☐	☐	☐
Irrigation / Sprinkler	☐	☐	☐
	☐	☐	☐
House Type	☐	☐	☐
Exterior Siding	☐	☐	☐
Deck / Patio / Porch	☐	☐	☐
Garage	☐	☐	☐
Window / Doors	☐	☐	☐
Roof / Gutters	☐	☐	☐
Fencing	☐	☐	☐

HOME SYSTEMS

	Good	Average	Poor
Electrical	☐	☐	☐
Air Conditioning / Fans	☐	☐	☐
Heating	☐	☐	☐
Security	☐	☐	☐
Plumbing	☐	☐	☐
Intercom	☐	☐	☐

FEATURES

	Good	Average	Poor
Home Warranty	☐	☐	☐
Energy Saving Features	☐	☐	☐

INTERIOR

	Good	Average	Poor
Walls / Trim / Ceilings	☐	☐	☐
Flooring	☐	☐	☐
Stairs	☐	☐	☐
Storage	☐	☐	☐
Living Room	☐	☐	☐
Family Room	☐	☐	☐
Dining Room	☐	☐	☐

	Good	Average	Poor
Master Bedroom	☐	☐	☐
Bedroom 2	☐	☐	☐
Bedroom 3	☐	☐	☐
Bedroom 4	☐	☐	☐
Master Bathroom	☐	☐	☐
Bathroom 2	☐	☐	☐
Bathroom 3	☐	☐	☐
Bonus / Game Room	☐	☐	☐

	Good	Average	Poor
Kitchen	☐	☐	☐
Cabinets	☐	☐	☐
Countertop	☐	☐	☐
Counter Space	☐	☐	☐
Flooring	☐	☐	☐
Oven / Stove	☐	☐	☐
Microwave	☐	☐	☐
Layout	☐	☐	☐
Light Fixtures	☐	☐	☐
Backsplash	☐	☐	☐
Pantry	☐	☐	☐
Appliances	☐	☐	☐
Island	☐	☐	☐

	Good	Average	Poor
Basement	☐	☐	☐
Garage	☐	☐	☐

COMMUNITY

	Good	Average	Poor
Immediate Neighborhood	☐	☐	☐
Close to Employment	☐	☐	☐
Close to Shopping	☐	☐	☐
Close to Transportation	☐	☐	☐
Close to Schools / Daycare	☐	☐	☐
Close to Places of Worship	☐	☐	☐
Near Recreational Facilities	☐	☐	☐
Close to Airport	☐	☐	☐
Near Police and Fire Department	☐	☐	☐

Address _____ Price _____

Bedrooms _____ Bathrooms _____ Sq.Ft. _____

Lot Size: _____ Year Built _____ School District _____

Annual Tax _____

EXTERIOR

	Good	Average	Poor
View/Yard/Landscaping	☐	☐	☐
Trees	☐	☐	☐
Lawn (Front)	☐	☐	☐
Lawn (Back)	☐	☐	☐
Fences (condition)	☐	☐	☐
Landscaping (condition)	☐	☐	☐
Irrigation / Sprinkler	☐	☐	☐
	☐	☐	☐
House Type	☐	☐	☐
Exterior Siding	☐	☐	☐
Deck / Patio / Porch	☐	☐	☐
Garage	☐	☐	☐
Window / Doors	☐	☐	☐
Roof / Gutters	☐	☐	☐
Fencing	☐	☐	☐

HOME SYSTEMS

	Good	Average	Poor
Electrical	☐	☐	☐
Air Conditioning / Fans	☐	☐	☐
Heating	☐	☐	☐
Security	☐	☐	☐
Plumbing	☐	☐	☐
Intercom	☐	☐	☐

FEATURES

	Good	Average	Poor
Home Warranty	☐	☐	☐
Energy Saving Features	☐	☐	☐

INTERIOR

	Good	Average	Poor
Walls / Trim / Ceilings	☐	☐	☐
Flooring	☐	☐	☐
Stairs	☐	☐	☐
Storage	☐	☐	☐
Living Room	☐	☐	☐
Family Room	☐	☐	☐
Dining Room	☐	☐	☐

	Good	Average	Poor
Master Bedroom	☐	☐	☐
Bedroom 2	☐	☐	☐
Bedroom 3	☐	☐	☐
Bedroom 4	☐	☐	☐
Master Bathroom	☐	☐	☐
Bathroom 2	☐	☐	☐
Bathroom 3	☐	☐	☐
Bonus / Game Room	☐	☐	☐

	Good	Average	Poor
Kitchen	☐	☐	☐
Cabinets	☐	☐	☐
Countertop	☐	☐	☐
Counter Space	☐	☐	☐
Flooring	☐	☐	☐
Oven / Stove	☐	☐	☐
Microwave	☐	☐	☐
Layout	☐	☐	☐
Light Fixtures	☐	☐	☐
Backsplash	☐	☐	☐
Pantry	☐	☐	☐
Appliances	☐	☐	☐
Island	☐	☐	☐

	Good	Average	Poor
Basement	☐	☐	☐
Garage	☐	☐	☐

COMMUNITY

	Good	Average	Poor
Immediate Neighborhood	☐	☐	☐
Close to Employment	☐	☐	☐
Close to Shopping	☐	☐	☐
Close to Transportation	☐	☐	☐
Close to Schools / Daycare	☐	☐	☐
Close to Places of Worship	☐	☐	☐
Near Recreational Facilities	☐	☐	☐
Close to Airport	☐	☐	☐
Near Police and Fire Department	☐	☐	☐

Address _____ Price _____

Bedrooms _____ Bathrooms _____ Sq.Ft. _____

Lot Size: _____ Year Built _____ School District _____

Annual Tax _____

EXTERIOR

	Good	Average	Poor
View/Yard/Landscaping	☐	☐	☐
Trees	☐	☐	☐
Lawn (Front)	☐	☐	☐
Lawn (Back)	☐	☐	☐
Fences (condition)	☐	☐	☐
Landscaping (condition)	☐	☐	☐
Irrigation / Sprinkler	☐	☐	☐
House Type	☐	☐	☐
Exterior Siding	☐	☐	☐
Deck / Patio / Porch	☐	☐	☐
Garage	☐	☐	☐
Window / Doors	☐	☐	☐
Roof / Gutters	☐	☐	☐
Fencing	☐	☐	☐

HOME SYSTEMS

	Good	Average	Poor
Electrical	☐	☐	☐
Air Conditioning / Fans	☐	☐	☐
Heating	☐	☐	☐
Security	☐	☐	☐
Plumbing	☐	☐	☐
Intercom	☐	☐	☐

FEATURES

	Good	Average	Poor
Home Warranty	☐	☐	☐
Energy Saving Features	☐	☐	☐

INTERIOR

	Good	Average	Poor
Walls / Trim / Ceilings	☐	☐	☐
Flooring	☐	☐	☐
Stairs	☐	☐	☐
Storage	☐	☐	☐
Living Room	☐	☐	☐
Family Room	☐	☐	☐
Dining Room	☐	☐	☐

	Good	Average	Poor
Master Bedroom	☐	☐	☐
Bedroom 2	☐	☐	☐
Bedroom 3	☐	☐	☐
Bedroom 4	☐	☐	☐
Master Bathroom	☐	☐	☐
Bathroom 2	☐	☐	☐
Bathroom 3	☐	☐	☐
Bonus / Game Room	☐	☐	☐

	Good	Average	Poor
Kitchen	☐	☐	
Cabinets	☐	☐	☐
Countertop	☐	☐	☐
Counter Space	☐	☐	☐
Flooring	☐	☐	☐
Oven / Stove	☐	☐	☐
Microwave	☐	☐	☐
Layout	☐	☐	☐
Light Fixtures	☐	☐	☐
Backsplash	☐	☐	☐
Pantry	☐	☐	☐
Appliances	☐	☐	☐
Island	☐	☐	☐

	Good	Average	Poor
Basement	☐	☐	☐
Garage	☐	☐	☐

COMMUNITY

	Good	Average	Poor
Immediate Neighborhood	☐	☐	☐
Close to Employment	☐	☐	☐
Close to Shopping	☐	☐	☐
Close to Transportation	☐	☐	☐
Close to Schools / Daycare	☐	☐	☐
Close to Places of Worship	☐	☐	☐
Near Recreational Facilities	☐	☐	☐
Close to Airport	☐	☐	☐
Near Police and Fire Department	☐	☐	☐

Address _____ Price _____

Bedrooms _____ Bathrooms _____ Sq.Ft. _____

Lot Size: _____ Year Built _____ School District _____

Annual Tax _____

EXTERIOR

	Good	Average	Poor
View/Yard/Landscaping	☐	☐	☐
Trees	☐	☐	☐
Lawn (Front)	☐	☐	☐
Lawn (Back)	☐	☐	☐
Fences (condition)	☐	☐	☐
Landscaping (condition)	☐	☐	☐
Irrigation / Sprinkler	☐	☐	☐
	☐	☐	☐
House Type	☐	☐	☐
Exterior Siding	☐	☐	☐
Deck / Patio / Porch	☐	☐	☐
Garage	☐	☐	☐
Window / Doors	☐	☐	☐
Roof / Gutters	☐	☐	☐
Fencing	☐	☐	☐

HOME SYSTEMS

	Good	Average	Poor
Electrical	☐	☐	☐
Air Conditioning / Fans	☐	☐	☐
Heating	☐	☐	☐
Security	☐	☐	☐
Plumbing	☐	☐	☐
Intercom	☐	☐	☐

FEATURES

	Good	Average	Poor
Home Warranty	☐	☐	☐
Energy Saving Features	☐	☐	☐

INTERIOR

	Good	Average	Poor
Walls / Trim / Ceilings	☐	☐	☐
Flooring	☐	☐	☐
Stairs	☐	☐	☐
Storage	☐	☐	☐
Living Room	☐	☐	☐
Family Room	☐	☐	☐
Dining Room	☐	☐	☐

	Good	Average	Poor
Master Bedroom	☐	☐	☐
Bedroom 2	☐	☐	☐
Bedroom 3	☐	☐	☐
Bedroom 4	☐	☐	☐
Master Bathroom	☐	☐	☐
Bathroom 2	☐	☐	☐
Bathroom 3	☐	☐	☐
Bonus / Game Room	☐	☐	☐

	Good	Average	Poor
Kitchen			
Cabinets	☐	☐	☐
Countertop	☐	☐	☐
Counter Space	☐	☐	☐
Flooring	☐	☐	☐
Oven / Stove	☐	☐	☐
Microwave	☐	☐	☐
Layout	☐	☐	☐
Light Fixtures	☐	☐	☐
Backsplash	☐	☐	☐
Pantry	☐	☐	☐
Appliances	☐	☐	☐
Island	☐	☐	☐

	Good	Average	Poor
Basement	☐	☐	☐
Garage	☐	☐	☐

COMMUNITY

	Good	Average	Poor
Immediate Neighborhood	☐	☐	☐
Close to Employment	☐	☐	☐
Close to Shopping	☐	☐	☐
Close to Transportation	☐	☐	☐
Close to Schools / Daycare	☐	☐	☐
Close to Places of Worship	☐	☐	☐
Near Recreational Facilities	☐	☐	☐
Close to Airport	☐	☐	☐
Near Police and Fire Department	☐	☐	☐

Address _____ Price _____

Bedrooms _____ Bathrooms _____ Sq.Ft. _____

Lot Size: _____ Year Built _____ School District _____

Annual Tax _____

EXTERIOR

	Good	Average	Poor
View/Yard/Landscaping	☐	☐	☐
Trees	☐	☐	☐
Lawn (Front)	☐	☐	☐
Lawn (Back)	☐	☐	☐
Fences (condition)	☐	☐	☐
Landscaping (condition)	☐	☐	☐
Irrigation / Sprinkler	☐	☐	☐
	☐	☐	☐
House Type	☐	☐	☐
Exterior Siding	☐	☐	☐
Deck / Patio / Porch	☐	☐	☐
Garage	☐	☐	☐
Window / Doors	☐	☐	☐
Roof / Gutters	☐	☐	☐
Fencing	☐	☐	☐

HOME SYSTEMS

	Good	Average	Poor
Electrical	☐	☐	☐
Air Conditioning / Fans	☐	☐	☐
Heating	☐	☐	☐
Security	☐	☐	☐
Plumbing	☐	☐	☐
Intercom	☐	☐	☐

FEATURES

	Good	Average	Poor
Home Warranty	☐	☐	☐
Energy Saving Features	☐	☐	☐

INTERIOR

	Good	Average	Poor
Walls / Trim / Ceilings	☐	☐	☐
Flooring	☐	☐	☐
Stairs	☐	☐	☐
Storage	☐	☐	☐
Living Room	☐	☐	☐
Family Room	☐	☐	☐
Dining Room	☐	☐	☐

	Good	Average	Poor
Master Bedroom	☐	☐	☐
Bedroom 2	☐	☐	☐
Bedroom 3	☐	☐	☐
Bedroom 4	☐	☐	☐
Master Bathroom	☐	☐	☐
Bathroom 2	☐	☐	☐
Bathroom 3	☐	☐	☐
Bonus / Game Room	☐	☐	☐

	Good	Average	Poor
Kitchen			
Cabinets	☐	☐	☐
Countertop	☐	☐	☐
Counter Space	☐	☐	☐
Flooring	☐	☐	☐
Oven / Stove	☐	☐	☐
Microwave	☐	☐	☐
Layout	☐	☐	☐
Light Fixtures	☐	☐	☐
Backsplash	☐	☐	☐
Pantry	☐	☐	☐
Appliances	☐	☐	☐
Island	☐	☐	☐

	Good	Average	Poor
Basement	☐	☐	☐
Garage	☐	☐	☐

COMMUNITY

	Good	Average	Poor
Immediate Neighborhood	☐	☐	☐
Close to Employment	☐	☐	☐
Close to Shopping	☐	☐	☐
Close to Transportation	☐	☐	☐
Close to Schools / Daycare	☐	☐	☐
Close to Places of Worship	☐	☐	☐
Near Recreational Facilities	☐	☐	☐
Close to Airport	☐	☐	☐
Near Police and Fire Department	☐	☐	☐

Address _____ Price _____

Bedrooms _____ Bathrooms _____ Sq.Ft. _____

Lot Size: _____ Year Built _____ School District _____

Annual Tax _____

EXTERIOR

	Good	Average	Poor
View/Yard/Landscaping	☐	☐	☐
Trees	☐	☐	☐
Lawn (Front)	☐	☐	☐
Lawn (Back)	☐	☐	☐
Fences (condition)	☐	☐	☐
Landscaping (condition)	☐	☐	☐
Irrigation / Sprinkler	☐	☐	☐
	☐	☐	☐
House Type	☐	☐	☐
Exterior Siding	☐	☐	☐
Deck / Patio / Porch	☐	☐	☐
Garage	☐	☐	☐
Window / Doors	☐	☐	☐
Roof / Gutters	☐	☐	☐
Fencing	☐	☐	☐

HOME SYSTEMS

	Good	Average	Poor
Electrical	☐	☐	☐
Air Conditioning / Fans	☐	☐	☐
Heating	☐	☐	☐
Security	☐	☐	☐
Plumbing	☐	☐	☐
Intercom	☐	☐	☐

FEATURES

	Good	Average	Poor
Home Warranty	☐	☐	☐
Energy Saving Features	☐	☐	☐

INTERIOR

	Good	Average	Poor
Walls / Trim / Ceilings	☐	☐	☐
Flooring	☐	☐	☐
Stairs	☐	☐	☐
Storage	☐	☐	☐
Living Room	☐	☐	☐
Family Room	☐	☐	☐
Dining Room	☐	☐	☐

	Good	Average	Poor
Master Bedroom	☐	☐	☐
Bedroom 2	☐	☐	☐
Bedroom 3	☐	☐	☐
Bedroom 4	☐	☐	☐
Master Bathroom	☐	☐	☐
Bathroom 2	☐	☐	☐
Bathroom 3	☐	☐	☐
Bonus / Game Room	☐	☐	☐

	Good	Average	Poor
Kitchen	☐	☐	☐
Cabinets	☐	☐	☐
Countertop	☐	☐	☐
Counter Space	☐	☐	☐
Flooring	☐	☐	☐
Oven / Stove	☐	☐	☐
Microwave	☐	☐	☐
Layout	☐	☐	☐
Light Fixtures	☐	☐	☐
Backsplash	☐	☐	☐
Pantry	☐	☐	☐
Appliances	☐	☐	☐
Island	☐	☐	☐

	Good	Average	Poor
Basement	☐	☐	☐
Garage	☐	☐	☐

COMMUNITY

	Good	Average	Poor
Immediate Neighborhood	☐	☐	☐
Close to Employment	☐	☐	☐
Close to Shopping	☐	☐	☐
Close to Transportation	☐	☐	☐
Close to Schools / Daycare	☐	☐	☐
Close to Places of Worship	☐	☐	☐
Near Recreational Facilities	☐	☐	☐
Close to Airport	☐	☐	☐
Near Police and Fire Department	☐	☐	☐

Address _____ Price _____

Bedrooms _____ Bathrooms _____ Sq.Ft. _____

Lot Size: _____ Year Built _____ School District _____

Annual Tax _____

EXTERIOR

	Good	Average	Poor
View/Yard/Landscaping	☐	☐	☐
Trees	☐	☐	☐
Lawn (Front)	☐	☐	☐
Lawn (Back)	☐	☐	☐
Fences (condition)	☐	☐	☐
Landscaping (condition)	☐	☐	☐
Irrigation / Sprinkler	☐	☐	☐
	☐	☐	☐
House Type	☐	☐	☐
Exterior Siding	☐	☐	☐
Deck / Patio / Porch	☐	☐	☐
Garage	☐	☐	☐
Window / Doors	☐	☐	☐
Roof / Gutters	☐	☐	☐
Fencing	☐	☐	☐

HOME SYSTEMS

	Good	Average	Poor
Electrical	☐	☐	☐
Air Conditioning / Fans	☐	☐	☐
Heating	☐	☐	☐
Security	☐	☐	☐
Plumbing	☐	☐	☐
Intercom	☐	☐	☐

FEATURES

	Good	Average	Poor
Home Warranty	☐	☐	☐
Energy Saving Features	☐	☐	☐

INTERIOR

	Good	Average	Poor
Walls / Trim / Ceilings	☐	☐	☐
Flooring	☐	☐	☐
Stairs	☐	☐	☐
Storage	☐	☐	☐
Living Room	☐	☐	☐
Family Room	☐	☐	☐
Dining Room	☐	☐	☐

	Good	Average	Poor
Master Bedroom	☐	☐	☐
Bedroom 2	☐	☐	☐
Bedroom 3	☐	☐	☐
Bedroom 4	☐	☐	☐
Master Bathroom	☐	☐	☐
Bathroom 2	☐	☐	☐
Bathroom 3	☐	☐	☐
Bonus / Game Room	☐	☐	☐

	Good	Average	Poor
Kitchen			
Cabinets	☐	☐	☐
Countertop	☐	☐	☐
Counter Space	☐	☐	☐
Flooring	☐	☐	☐
Oven / Stove	☐	☐	☐
Microwave	☐	☐	☐
Layout	☐	☐	☐
Light Fixtures	☐	☐	☐
Backsplash	☐	☐	☐
Pantry	☐	☐	☐
Appliances	☐	☐	☐
Island	☐	☐	☐

	Good	Average	Poor
Basement	☐	☐	☐
Garage	☐	☐	☐

COMMUNITY

	Good	Average	Poor
Immediate Neighborhood	☐	☐	☐
Close to Employment	☐	☐	☐
Close to Shopping	☐	☐	☐
Close to Transportation	☐	☐	☐
Close to Schools / Daycare	☐	☐	☐
Close to Places of Worship	☐	☐	☐
Near Recreational Facilities	☐	☐	☐
Close to Airport	☐	☐	☐
Near Police and Fire Department	☐	☐	☐

Address _____ Price _____

Bedrooms _____ Bathrooms _____ Sq.Ft. _____

Lot Size: _____ Year Built _____ School District _____

Annual Tax _____

EXTERIOR

	Good	Average	Poor
View/Yard/Landscaping	☐	☐	☐
Trees	☐	☐	☐
Lawn (Front)	☐	☐	☐
Lawn (Back)	☐	☐	☐
Fences (condition)	☐	☐	☐
Landscaping (condition)	☐	☐	☐
Irrigation / Sprinkler	☐	☐	☐
	☐	☐	☐
House Type	☐	☐	☐
Exterior Siding	☐	☐	☐
Deck / Patio / Porch	☐	☐	☐
Garage	☐	☐	☐
Window / Doors	☐	☐	☐
Roof / Gutters	☐	☐	☐
Fencing	☐	☐	☐

HOME SYSTEMS

	Good	Average	Poor
Electrical	☐	☐	☐
Air Conditioning / Fans	☐	☐	☐
Heating	☐	☐	☐
Security	☐	☐	☐
Plumbing	☐	☐	☐
Intercom	☐	☐	☐

FEATURES

	Good	Average	Poor
Home Warranty	☐	☐	☐
Energy Saving Features	☐	☐	☐

INTERIOR

	Good	Average	Poor
Walls / Trim / Ceilings	☐	☐	☐
Flooring	☐	☐	☐
Stairs	☐	☐	☐
Storage	☐	☐	☐
Living Room	☐	☐	☐
Family Room	☐	☐	☐
Dining Room	☐	☐	☐

	Good	Average	Poor
Master Bedroom	☐	☐	☐
Bedroom 2	☐	☐	☐
Bedroom 3	☐	☐	☐
Bedroom 4	☐	☐	☐
Master Bathroom	☐	☐	☐
Bathroom 2	☐	☐	☐
Bathroom 3	☐	☐	☐
Bonus / Game Room	☐	☐	☐

	Good	Average	Poor
Kitchen	☐	☐	☐
Cabinets	☐	☐	☐
Countertop	☐	☐	☐
Counter Space	☐	☐	☐
Flooring	☐	☐	☐
Oven / Stove	☐	☐	☐
Microwave	☐	☐	☐
Layout	☐	☐	☐
Light Fixtures	☐	☐	☐
Backsplash	☐	☐	☐
Pantry	☐	☐	☐
Appliances	☐	☐	☐
Island	☐	☐	☐

	Good	Average	Poor
Basement	☐	☐	☐
Garage	☐	☐	☐

COMMUNITY

	Good	Average	Poor
Immediate Neighborhood	☐	☐	☐
Close to Employment	☐	☐	☐
Close to Shopping	☐	☐	☐
Close to Transportation	☐	☐	☐
Close to Schools / Daycare	☐	☐	☐
Close to Places of Worship	☐	☐	☐
Near Recreational Facilities	☐	☐	☐
Close to Airport	☐	☐	☐
Near Police and Fire Department	☐	☐	☐

Address _____ Price _____

Bedrooms _____ Bathrooms _____ Sq.Ft. _____

Lot Size: _____ Year Built _____ School District _____

Annual Tax _____

EXTERIOR

	Good	Average	Poor
View/Yard/Landscaping	☐	☐	☐
Trees	☐	☐	☐
Lawn (Front)	☐	☐	☐
Lawn (Back)	☐	☐	☐
Fences (condition)	☐	☐	☐
Landscaping (condition)	☐	☐	☐
Irrigation / Sprinkler	☐	☐	☐
	☐	☐	☐
House Type	☐	☐	☐
Exterior Siding	☐	☐	☐
Deck / Patio / Porch	☐	☐	☐
Garage	☐	☐	☐
Window / Doors	☐	☐	☐
Roof / Gutters	☐	☐	☐
Fencing	☐	☐	☐

HOME SYSTEMS

	Good	Average	Poor
Electrical	☐	☐	☐
Air Conditioning / Fans	☐	☐	☐
Heating	☐	☐	☐
Security	☐	☐	☐
Plumbing	☐	☐	☐
Intercom	☐	☐	☐

FEATURES

	Good	Average	Poor
Home Warranty	☐	☐	☐
Energy Saving Features	☐	☐	☐

INTERIOR

	Good	Average	Poor
Walls / Trim / Ceilings	☐	☐	☐
Flooring	☐	☐	☐
Stairs	☐	☐	☐
Storage	☐	☐	☐
Living Room	☐	☐	☐
Family Room	☐	☐	☐
Dining Room	☐	☐	☐

	Good	Average	Poor
Master Bedroom	☐	☐	☐
Bedroom 2	☐	☐	☐
Bedroom 3	☐	☐	☐
Bedroom 4	☐	☐	☐
Master Bathroom	☐	☐	☐
Bathroom 2	☐	☐	☐
Bathroom 3	☐	☐	☐
Bonus / Game Room	☐	☐	☐

	Good	Average	Poor
Kitchen	☐	☐	☐
Cabinets	☐	☐	☐
Countertop	☐	☐	☐
Counter Space	☐	☐	☐
Flooring	☐	☐	☐
Oven / Stove	☐	☐	☐
Microwave	☐	☐	☐
Layout	☐	☐	☐
Light Fixtures	☐	☐	☐
Backsplash	☐	☐	☐
Pantry	☐	☐	☐
Appliances	☐	☐	☐
Island	☐	☐	☐

	Good	Average	Poor
Basement	☐	☐	☐
Garage	☐	☐	☐

COMMUNITY

	Good	Average	Poor
Immediate Neighborhood	☐	☐	☐
Close to Employment	☐	☐	☐
Close to Shopping	☐	☐	☐
Close to Transportation	☐	☐	☐
Close to Schools / Daycare	☐	☐	☐
Close to Places of Worship	☐	☐	☐
Near Recreational Facilities	☐	☐	☐
Close to Airport	☐	☐	☐
Near Police and Fire Department	☐	☐	☐

Address _____   Price _____

Bedrooms _____   Bathrooms _____   Sq.Ft. _____

Lot Size: _____   Year Built _____   School District _____

Annual Tax _____

EXTERIOR

	Good	Average	Poor
View/Yard/Landscaping	☐	☐	☐
Trees	☐	☐	☐
Lawn (Front)	☐	☐	☐
Lawn (Back)	☐	☐	☐
Fences (condition)	☐	☐	☐
Landscaping (condition)	☐	☐	☐
Irrigation / Sprinkler	☐	☐	☐
	☐	☐	☐
House Type	☐	☐	☐
Exterior Siding	☐	☐	☐
Deck / Patio / Porch	☐	☐	☐
Garage	☐	☐	☐
Window / Doors	☐	☐	☐
Roof / Gutters	☐	☐	☐
Fencing	☐	☐	☐

HOME SYSTEMS

	Good	Average	Poor
Electrical	☐	☐	☐
Air Conditioning / Fans	☐	☐	☐
Heating	☐	☐	☐
Security	☐	☐	☐
Plumbing	☐	☐	☐
Intercom	☐	☐	☐

FEATURES

	Good	Average	Poor
Home Warranty	☐	☐	☐
Energy Saving Features	☐	☐	☐

INTERIOR

	Good	Average	Poor
Walls / Trim / Ceilings	☐	☐	☐
Flooring	☐	☐	☐
Stairs	☐	☐	☐
Storage	☐	☐	☐
Living Room	☐	☐	☐
Family Room	☐	☐	☐
Dining Room	☐	☐	☐

	Good	Average	Poor
Master Bedroom	☐	☐	☐
Bedroom 2	☐	☐	☐
Bedroom 3	☐	☐	☐
Bedroom 4	☐	☐	☐
Master Bathroom	☐	☐	☐
Bathroom 2	☐	☐	☐
Bathroom 3	☐	☐	☐
Bonus / Game Room	☐	☐	☐

	Good	Average	Poor
Kitchen	☐	☐	☐
Cabinets	☐	☐	☐
Countertop	☐	☐	☐
Counter Space	☐	☐	☐
Flooring	☐	☐	☐
Oven / Stove	☐	☐	☐
Microwave	☐	☐	☐
Layout	☐	☐	☐
Light Fixtures	☐	☐	☐
Backsplash	☐	☐	☐
Pantry	☐	☐	☐
Appliances	☐	☐	☐
Island	☐	☐	☐

	Good	Average	Poor
Basement	☐	☐	☐
Garage	☐	☐	☐

COMMUNITY

	Good	Average	Poor
Immediate Neighborhood	☐	☐	☐
Close to Employment	☐	☐	☐
Close to Shopping	☐	☐	☐
Close to Transportation	☐	☐	☐
Close to Schools / Daycare	☐	☐	☐
Close to Places of Worship	☐	☐	☐
Near Recreational Facilities	☐	☐	☐
Close to Airport	☐	☐	☐
Near Police and Fire Department	☐	☐	☐

Address _____ Price _____

Bedrooms _____ Bathrooms _____ Sq.Ft. _____

Lot Size: _____ Year Built _____ School District _____

Annual Tax _____

EXTERIOR

	Good	Average	Poor
View/Yard/Landscaping	☐	☐	☐
Trees	☐	☐	☐
Lawn (Front)	☐	☐	☐
Lawn (Back)	☐	☐	☐
Fences (condition)	☐	☐	☐
Landscaping (condition)	☐	☐	☐
Irrigation / Sprinkler	☐	☐	☐
	☐	☐	☐
House Type	☐	☐	☐
Exterior Siding	☐	☐	☐
Deck / Patio / Porch	☐	☐	☐
Garage	☐	☐	☐
Window / Doors	☐	☐	☐
Roof / Gutters	☐	☐	☐
Fencing	☐	☐	☐

HOME SYSTEMS

	Good	Average	Poor
Electrical	☐	☐	☐
Air Conditioning / Fans	☐	☐	☐
Heating	☐	☐	☐
Security	☐	☐	☐
Plumbing	☐	☐	☐
Intercom	☐	☐	☐

FEATURES

	Good	Average	Poor
Home Warranty	☐	☐	☐
Energy Saving Features	☐	☐	☐

INTERIOR

	Good	Average	Poor
Walls / Trim / Ceilings	☐	☐	☐
Flooring	☐	☐	☐
Stairs	☐	☐	☐
Storage	☐	☐	☐
Living Room	☐	☐	☐
Family Room	☐	☐	☐
Dining Room	☐	☐	☐

	Good	Average	Poor
Master Bedroom	☐	☐	☐
Bedroom 2	☐	☐	☐
Bedroom 3	☐	☐	☐
Bedroom 4	☐	☐	☐
Master Bathroom	☐	☐	☐
Bathroom 2	☐	☐	☐
Bathroom 3	☐	☐	☐
Bonus / Game Room	☐	☐	☐

	Good	Average	Poor
Kitchen			
Cabinets	☐	☐	☐
Countertop	☐	☐	☐
Counter Space	☐	☐	☐
Flooring	☐	☐	☐
Oven / Stove	☐	☐	☐
Microwave	☐	☐	☐
Layout	☐	☐	☐
Light Fixtures	☐	☐	☐
Backsplash	☐	☐	☐
Pantry	☐	☐	☐
Appliances	☐	☐	☐
Island	☐	☐	☐

	Good	Average	Poor
Basement	☐	☐	☐
Garage	☐	☐	☐

COMMUNITY

	Good	Average	Poor
Immediate Neighborhood	☐	☐	☐
Close to Employment	☐	☐	☐
Close to Shopping	☐	☐	☐
Close to Transportation	☐	☐	☐
Close to Schools / Daycare	☐	☐	☐
Close to Places of Worship	☐	☐	☐
Near Recreational Facilities	☐	☐	☐
Close to Airport	☐	☐	☐
Near Police and Fire Department	☐	☐	☐

Address _____ Price _____

Bedrooms _____ Bathrooms _____ Sq.Ft. _____

Lot Size: _____ Year Built _____ School District _____

Annual Tax _____

EXTERIOR

	Good	Average	Poor
View/Yard/Landscaping	☐	☐	☐
Trees	☐	☐	☐
Lawn (Front)	☐	☐	☐
Lawn (Back)	☐	☐	☐
Fences (condition)	☐	☐	☐
Landscaping (condition)	☐	☐	☐
Irrigation / Sprinkler	☐	☐	☐
	☐	☐	☐
House Type	☐	☐	☐
Exterior Siding	☐	☐	☐
Deck / Patio / Porch	☐	☐	☐
Garage	☐	☐	☐
Window / Doors	☐	☐	☐
Roof / Gutters	☐	☐	☐
Fencing	☐	☐	☐

HOME SYSTEMS

	Good	Average	Poor
Electrical	☐	☐	☐
Air Conditioning / Fans	☐	☐	☐
Heating	☐	☐	☐
Security	☐	☐	☐
Plumbing	☐	☐	☐
Intercom	☐	☐	☐

FEATURES

	Good	Average	Poor
Home Warranty	☐	☐	☐
Energy Saving Features	☐	☐	☐

INTERIOR

	Good	Average	Poor
Walls / Trim / Ceilings	☐	☐	☐
Flooring	☐	☐	☐
Stairs	☐	☐	☐
Storage	☐	☐	☐
Living Room	☐	☐	☐
Family Room	☐	☐	☐
Dining Room	☐	☐	☐

	Good	Average	Poor
Master Bedroom	☐	☐	☐
Bedroom 2	☐	☐	☐
Bedroom 3	☐	☐	☐
Bedroom 4	☐	☐	☐
Master Bathroom	☐	☐	☐
Bathroom 2	☐	☐	☐
Bathroom 3	☐	☐	☐
Bonus / Game Room	☐	☐	☐

	Good	Average	Poor
Kitchen	☐	☐	☐
Cabinets	☐	☐	☐
Countertop	☐	☐	☐
Counter Space	☐	☐	☐
Flooring	☐	☐	☐
Oven / Stove	☐	☐	☐
Microwave	☐	☐	☐
Layout	☐	☐	☐
Light Fixtures	☐	☐	☐
Backsplash	☐	☐	☐
Pantry	☐	☐	☐
Appliances	☐	☐	☐
Island	☐	☐	☐

	Good	Average	Poor
Basement	☐	☐	☐
Garage	☐	☐	☐

COMMUNITY

	Good	Average	Poor
Immediate Neighborhood	☐	☐	☐
Close to Employment	☐	☐	☐
Close to Shopping	☐	☐	☐
Close to Transportation	☐	☐	☐
Close to Schools / Daycare	☐	☐	☐
Close to Places of Worship	☐	☐	☐
Near Recreational Facilities	☐	☐	☐
Close to Airport	☐	☐	☐
Near Police and Fire Department	☐	☐	☐

Address _____ Price _____

Bedrooms _____ Bathrooms _____ Sq.Ft. _____

Lot Size: _____ Year Built _____ School District _____

Annual Tax _____

EXTERIOR

	Good	Average	Poor
View/Yard/Landscaping	☐	☐	☐
Trees	☐	☐	☐
Lawn (Front)	☐	☐	☐
Lawn (Back)	☐	☐	☐
Fences (condition)	☐	☐	☐
Landscaping (condition)	☐	☐	☐
Irrigation / Sprinkler	☐	☐	☐
House Type	☐	☐	☐
Exterior Siding	☐	☐	☐
Deck / Patio / Porch	☐	☐	☐
Garage	☐	☐	☐
Window / Doors	☐	☐	☐
Roof / Gutters	☐	☐	☐
Fencing	☐	☐	☐

HOME SYSTEMS

	Good	Average	Poor
Electrical	☐	☐	☐
Air Conditioning / Fans	☐	☐	☐
Heating	☐	☐	☐
Security	☐	☐	☐
Plumbing	☐	☐	☐
Intercom	☐	☐	☐

FEATURES

	Good	Average	Poor
Home Warranty	☐	☐	☐
Energy Saving Features	☐	☐	☐

INTERIOR

	Good	Average	Poor
Walls / Trim / Ceilings	☐	☐	☐
Flooring	☐	☐	☐
Stairs	☐	☐	☐
Storage	☐	☐	☐
Living Room	☐	☐	☐
Family Room	☐	☐	☐
Dining Room	☐	☐	☐

	Good	Average	Poor
Master Bedroom	☐	☐	☐
Bedroom 2	☐	☐	☐
Bedroom 3	☐	☐	☐
Bedroom 4	☐	☐	☐
Master Bathroom	☐	☐	☐
Bathroom 2	☐	☐	☐
Bathroom 3	☐	☐	☐
Bonus / Game Room	☐	☐	☐

	Good	Average	Poor
Kitchen	☐	☐	
Cabinets	☐	☐	☐
Countertop	☐	☐	☐
Counter Space	☐	☐	☐
Flooring	☐	☐	☐
Oven / Stove	☐	☐	☐
Microwave	☐	☐	☐
Layout	☐	☐	☐
Light Fixtures	☐	☐	☐
Backsplash	☐	☐	☐
Pantry	☐	☐	☐
Appliances	☐	☐	☐
Island	☐	☐	☐

	Good	Average	Poor
Basement	☐	☐	☐
Garage	☐	☐	☐

COMMUNITY

	Good	Average	Poor
Immediate Neighborhood	☐	☐	☐
Close to Employment	☐	☐	☐
Close to Shopping	☐	☐	☐
Close to Transportation	☐	☐	☐
Close to Schools / Daycare	☐	☐	☐
Close to Places of Worship	☐	☐	☐
Near Recreational Facilities	☐	☐	☐
Close to Airport	☐	☐	☐
Near Police and Fire Department	☐	☐	☐

Address _____ Price _____

Bedrooms _____ Bathrooms _____ Sq.Ft. _____

Lot Size: _____ Year Built _____ School District _____

Annual Tax _____

EXTERIOR

	Good	Average	Poor
View/Yard/Landscaping	☐	☐	☐
Trees	☐	☐	☐
Lawn (Front)	☐	☐	☐
Lawn (Back)	☐	☐	☐
Fences (condition)	☐	☐	☐
Landscaping (condition)	☐	☐	☐
Irrigation / Sprinkler	☐	☐	☐
	☐	☐	☐
House Type	☐	☐	☐
Exterior Siding	☐	☐	☐
Deck / Patio / Porch	☐	☐	☐
Garage	☐	☐	☐
Window / Doors	☐	☐	☐
Roof / Gutters	☐	☐	☐
Fencing	☐	☐	☐

HOME SYSTEMS

	Good	Average	Poor
Electrical	☐	☐	☐
Air Conditioning / Fans	☐	☐	☐
Heating	☐	☐	☐
Security	☐	☐	☐
Plumbing	☐	☐	☐
Intercom	☐	☐	☐

FEATURES

	Good	Average	Poor
Home Warranty	☐	☐	☐
Energy Saving Features	☐	☐	☐

INTERIOR

	Good	Average	Poor
Walls / Trim / Ceilings	☐	☐	☐
Flooring	☐	☐	☐
Stairs	☐	☐	☐
Storage	☐	☐	☐
Living Room	☐	☐	☐
Family Room	☐	☐	☐
Dining Room	☐	☐	☐

	Good	Average	Poor
Master Bedroom	☐	☐	☐
Bedroom 2	☐	☐	☐
Bedroom 3	☐	☐	☐
Bedroom 4	☐	☐	☐
Master Bathroom	☐	☐	☐
Bathroom 2	☐	☐	☐
Bathroom 3	☐	☐	☐
Bonus / Game Room	☐	☐	☐

	Good	Average	Poor
Kitchen	☐	☐	☐
Cabinets	☐	☐	☐
Countertop	☐	☐	☐
Counter Space	☐	☐	☐
Flooring	☐	☐	☐
Oven / Stove	☐	☐	☐
Microwave	☐	☐	☐
Layout	☐	☐	☐
Light Fixtures	☐	☐	☐
Backsplash	☐	☐	☐
Pantry	☐	☐	☐
Appliances	☐	☐	☐
Island	☐	☐	☐

	Good	Average	Poor
Basement	☐	☐	☐
Garage	☐	☐	☐

COMMUNITY

	Good	Average	Poor
Immediate Neighborhood	☐	☐	☐
Close to Employment	☐	☐	☐
Close to Shopping	☐	☐	☐
Close to Transportation	☐	☐	☐
Close to Schools / Daycare	☐	☐	☐
Close to Places of Worship	☐	☐	☐
Near Recreational Facilities	☐	☐	☐
Close to Airport	☐	☐	☐
Near Police and Fire Department	☐	☐	☐

Address _____ Price _____

Bedrooms _____ Bathrooms _____ Sq.Ft. _____

Lot Size: _____ Year Built _____ School District _____

Annual Tax _____

EXTERIOR

	Good	Average	Poor
View/Yard/Landscaping	☐	☐	☐
Trees	☐	☐	☐
Lawn (Front)	☐	☐	☐
Lawn (Back)	☐	☐	☐
Fences (condition)	☐	☐	☐
Landscaping (condition)	☐	☐	☐
Irrigation / Sprinkler	☐	☐	☐
	☐	☐	☐
House Type	☐	☐	☐
Exterior Siding	☐	☐	☐
Deck / Patio / Porch	☐	☐	☐
Garage	☐	☐	☐
Window / Doors	☐	☐	☐
Roof / Gutters	☐	☐	☐
Fencing	☐	☐	☐

HOME SYSTEMS

	Good	Average	Poor
Electrical	☐	☐	☐
Air Conditioning / Fans	☐	☐	☐
Heating	☐	☐	☐
Security	☐	☐	☐
Plumbing	☐	☐	☐
Intercom	☐	☐	☐

FEATURES

	Good	Average	Poor
Home Warranty	☐	☐	☐
Energy Saving Features	☐	☐	☐

INTERIOR

	Good	Average	Poor
Walls / Trim / Ceilings	☐	☐	☐
Flooring	☐	☐	☐
Stairs	☐	☐	☐
Storage	☐	☐	☐
Living Room	☐	☐	☐
Family Room	☐	☐	☐
Dining Room	☐	☐	☐

	Good	Average	Poor
Master Bedroom	☐	☐	☐
Bedroom 2	☐	☐	☐
Bedroom 3	☐	☐	☐
Bedroom 4	☐	☐	☐
Master Bathroom	☐	☐	☐
Bathroom 2	☐	☐	☐
Bathroom 3	☐	☐	☐
Bonus / Game Room	☐	☐	☐

	Good	Average	Poor
Kitchen	☐	☐	☐
Cabinets	☐	☐	☐
Countertop	☐	☐	☐
Counter Space	☐	☐	☐
Flooring	☐	☐	☐
Oven / Stove	☐	☐	☐
Microwave	☐	☐	☐
Layout	☐	☐	☐
Light Fixtures	☐	☐	☐
Backsplash	☐	☐	☐
Pantry	☐	☐	☐
Appliances	☐	☐	☐
Island	☐	☐	☐

	Good	Average	Poor
Basement	☐	☐	☐
Garage	☐	☐	☐

COMMUNITY

	Good	Average	Poor
Immediate Neighborhood	☐	☐	☐
Close to Employment	☐	☐	☐
Close to Shopping	☐	☐	☐
Close to Transportation	☐	☐	☐
Close to Schools / Daycare	☐	☐	☐
Close to Places of Worship	☐	☐	☐
Near Recreational Facilities	☐	☐	☐
Close to Airport	☐	☐	☐
Near Police and Fire Department	☐	☐	☐

Address _____ Price _____

Bedrooms _____ Bathrooms _____ Sq.Ft. _____

Lot Size: _____ Year Built _____ School District _____

Annual Tax _____

EXTERIOR

	Good	Average	Poor
View/Yard/Landscaping	☐	☐	☐
Trees	☐	☐	☐
Lawn (Front)	☐	☐	☐
Lawn (Back)	☐	☐	☐
Fences (condition)	☐	☐	☐
Landscaping (condition)	☐	☐	☐
Irrigation / Sprinkler	☐	☐	☐
	☐	☐	☐
House Type	☐	☐	☐
Exterior Siding	☐	☐	☐
Deck / Patio / Porch	☐	☐	☐
Garage	☐	☐	☐
Window / Doors	☐	☐	☐
Roof / Gutters	☐	☐	☐
Fencing	☐	☐	☐

HOME SYSTEMS

	Good	Average	Poor
Electrical	☐	☐	☐
Air Conditioning / Fans	☐	☐	☐
Heating	☐	☐	☐
Security	☐	☐	☐
Plumbing	☐	☐	☐
Intercom	☐	☐	☐

FEATURES

	Good	Average	Poor
Home Warranty	☐	☐	☐
Energy Saving Features	☐	☐	☐

INTERIOR

	Good	Average	Poor
Walls / Trim / Ceilings	☐	☐	☐
Flooring	☐	☐	☐
Stairs	☐	☐	☐
Storage	☐	☐	☐
Living Room	☐	☐	☐
Family Room	☐	☐	☐
Dining Room	☐	☐	☐

	Good	Average	Poor
Master Bedroom	☐	☐	☐
Bedroom 2	☐	☐	☐
Bedroom 3	☐	☐	☐
Bedroom 4	☐	☐	☐
Master Bathroom	☐	☐	☐
Bathroom 2	☐	☐	☐
Bathroom 3	☐	☐	☐
Bonus / Game Room	☐	☐	☐

	Good	Average	Poor
Kitchen	☐	☐	☐
Cabinets	☐	☐	☐
Countertop	☐	☐	☐
Counter Space	☐	☐	☐
Flooring	☐	☐	☐
Oven / Stove	☐	☐	☐
Microwave	☐	☐	☐
Layout	☐	☐	☐
Light Fixtures	☐	☐	☐
Backsplash	☐	☐	☐
Pantry	☐	☐	☐
Appliances	☐	☐	☐
Island	☐	☐	☐

	Good	Average	Poor
Basement	☐	☐	☐
Garage	☐	☐	☐

COMMUNITY

	Good	Average	Poor
Immediate Neighborhood	☐	☐	☐
Close to Employment	☐	☐	☐
Close to Shopping	☐	☐	☐
Close to Transportation	☐	☐	☐
Close to Schools / Daycare	☐	☐	☐
Close to Places of Worship	☐	☐	☐
Near Recreational Facilities	☐	☐	☐
Close to Airport	☐	☐	☐
Near Police and Fire Department	☐	☐	☐

Address _____   Price _____

Bedrooms _____   Bathrooms _____   Sq.Ft. _____

Lot Size: _____   Year Built _____   School District _____

Annual Tax _____

EXTERIOR

	Good	Average	Poor
View/Yard/Landscaping	☐	☐	☐
Trees	☐	☐	☐
Lawn (Front)	☐	☐	☐
Lawn (Back)	☐	☐	☐
Fences (condition)	☐	☐	☐
Landscaping (condition)	☐	☐	☐
Irrigation / Sprinkler	☐	☐	☐
	☐	☐	☐
House Type	☐	☐	☐
Exterior Siding	☐	☐	☐
Deck / Patio / Porch	☐	☐	☐
Garage	☐	☐	☐
Window / Doors	☐	☐	☐
Roof / Gutters	☐	☐	☐
Fencing	☐	☐	☐

HOME SYSTEMS

	Good	Average	Poor
Electrical	☐	☐	☐
Air Conditioning / Fans	☐	☐	☐
Heating	☐	☐	☐
Security	☐	☐	☐
Plumbing	☐	☐	☐
Intercom	☐	☐	☐

FEATURES

	Good	Average	Poor
Home Warranty	☐	☐	☐
Energy Saving Features	☐	☐	☐

INTERIOR

	Good	Average	Poor
Walls / Trim / Ceilings	☐	☐	☐
Flooring	☐	☐	☐
Stairs	☐	☐	☐
Storage	☐	☐	☐
Living Room	☐	☐	☐
Family Room	☐	☐	☐
Dining Room	☐	☐	☐

	Good	Average	Poor
Master Bedroom	☐	☐	☐
Bedroom 2	☐	☐	☐
Bedroom 3	☐	☐	☐
Bedroom 4	☐	☐	☐
Master Bathroom	☐	☐	☐
Bathroom 2	☐	☐	☐
Bathroom 3	☐	☐	☐
Bonus / Game Room	☐	☐	☐

	Good	Average	Poor
Kitchen			
Cabinets	☐	☐	☐
Countertop	☐	☐	☐
Counter Space	☐	☐	☐
Flooring	☐	☐	☐
Oven / Stove	☐	☐	☐
Microwave	☐	☐	☐
Layout	☐	☐	☐
Light Fixtures	☐	☐	☐
Backsplash	☐	☐	☐
Pantry	☐	☐	☐
Appliances	☐	☐	☐
Island	☐	☐	☐

	Good	Average	Poor
Basement	☐	☐	☐
Garage	☐	☐	☐

COMMUNITY

	Good	Average	Poor
Immediate Neighborhood	☐	☐	☐
Close to Employment	☐	☐	☐
Close to Shopping	☐	☐	☐
Close to Transportation	☐	☐	☐
Close to Schools / Daycare	☐	☐	☐
Close to Places of Worship	☐	☐	☐
Near Recreational Facilities	☐	☐	☐
Close to Airport	☐	☐	☐
Near Police and Fire Department	☐	☐	☐

Address _____ Price _____

Bedrooms _____ Bathrooms _____ Sq.Ft. _____

Lot Size: _____ Year Built _____ School District _____

Annual Tax _____

EXTERIOR

	Good	Average	Poor
View/Yard/Landscaping	☐	☐	☐
Trees	☐	☐	☐
Lawn (Front)	☐	☐	☐
Lawn (Back)	☐	☐	☐
Fences (condition)	☐	☐	☐
Landscaping (condition)	☐	☐	☐
Irrigation / Sprinkler	☐	☐	☐
	☐	☐	☐
House Type	☐	☐	☐
Exterior Siding	☐	☐	☐
Deck / Patio / Porch	☐	☐	☐
Garage	☐	☐	☐
Window / Doors	☐	☐	☐
Roof / Gutters	☐	☐	☐
Fencing	☐	☐	☐

HOME SYSTEMS

	Good	Average	Poor
Electrical	☐	☐	☐
Air Conditioning / Fans	☐	☐	☐
Heating	☐	☐	☐
Security	☐	☐	☐
Plumbing	☐	☐	☐
Intercom	☐	☐	☐

FEATURES

	Good	Average	Poor
Home Warranty	☐	☐	☐
Energy Saving Features	☐	☐	☐

INTERIOR

	Good	Average	Poor
Walls / Trim / Ceilings	☐	☐	☐
Flooring	☐	☐	☐
Stairs	☐	☐	☐
Storage	☐	☐	☐
Living Room	☐	☐	☐
Family Room	☐	☐	☐
Dining Room	☐	☐	☐

	Good	Average	Poor
Master Bedroom	☐	☐	☐
Bedroom 2	☐	☐	☐
Bedroom 3	☐	☐	☐
Bedroom 4	☐	☐	☐
Master Bathroom	☐	☐	☐
Bathroom 2	☐	☐	☐
Bathroom 3	☐	☐	☐
Bonus / Game Room	☐	☐	☐

	Good	Average	Poor
Kitchen	☐	☐	☐
Cabinets	☐	☐	☐
Countertop	☐	☐	☐
Counter Space	☐	☐	☐
Flooring	☐	☐	☐
Oven / Stove	☐	☐	☐
Microwave	☐	☐	☐
Layout	☐	☐	☐
Light Fixtures	☐	☐	☐
Backsplash	☐	☐	☐
Pantry	☐	☐	☐
Appliances	☐	☐	☐
Island	☐	☐	☐

	Good	Average	Poor
Basement	☐	☐	☐
Garage	☐	☐	☐

COMMUNITY

	Good	Average	Poor
Immediate Neighborhood	☐	☐	☐
Close to Employment	☐	☐	☐
Close to Shopping	☐	☐	☐
Close to Transportation	☐	☐	☐
Close to Schools / Daycare	☐	☐	☐
Close to Places of Worship	☐	☐	☐
Near Recreational Facilities	☐	☐	☐
Close to Airport	☐	☐	☐
Near Police and Fire Department	☐	☐	☐

Address _____   Price _____

Bedrooms _____   Bathrooms _____   Sq.Ft. _____

Lot Size: _____   Year Built _____   School District _____

Annual Tax _____

EXTERIOR

	Good	Average	Poor
View/Yard/Landscaping	☐	☐	☐
Trees	☐	☐	☐
Lawn (Front)	☐	☐	☐
Lawn (Back)	☐	☐	☐
Fences (condition)	☐	☐	☐
Landscaping (condition)	☐	☐	☐
Irrigation / Sprinkler	☐	☐	☐
House Type	☐	☐	☐
Exterior Siding	☐	☐	☐
Deck / Patio / Porch	☐	☐	☐
Garage	☐	☐	☐
Window / Doors	☐	☐	☐
Roof / Gutters	☐	☐	☐
Fencing	☐	☐	☐

HOME SYSTEMS

	Good	Average	Poor
Electrical	☐	☐	☐
Air Conditioning / Fans	☐	☐	☐
Heating	☐	☐	☐
Security	☐	☐	☐
Plumbing	☐	☐	☐
Intercom	☐	☐	☐

FEATURES

	Good	Average	Poor
Home Warranty	☐	☐	☐
Energy Saving Features	☐	☐	☐

INTERIOR

	Good	Average	Poor
Walls / Trim / Ceilings	☐	☐	☐
Flooring	☐	☐	☐
Stairs	☐	☐	☐
Storage	☐	☐	☐
Living Room	☐	☐	☐
Family Room	☐	☐	☐
Dining Room	☐	☐	☐

	Good	Average	Poor
Master Bedroom	☐	☐	☐
Bedroom 2	☐	☐	☐
Bedroom 3	☐	☐	☐
Bedroom 4	☐	☐	☐
Master Bathroom	☐	☐	☐
Bathroom 2	☐	☐	☐
Bathroom 3	☐	☐	☐
Bonus / Game Room	☐	☐	☐
	Good	Average	Poor
Kitchen			
Cabinets	☐	☐	☐
Countertop	☐	☐	☐
Counter Space	☐	☐	☐
Flooring	☐	☐	☐
Oven / Stove	☐	☐	☐
Microwave	☐	☐	☐
Layout	☐	☐	☐
Light Fixtures	☐	☐	☐
Backsplash	☐	☐	☐
Pantry	☐	☐	☐
Appliances	☐	☐	☐
Island	☐	☐	☐
	Good	Average	Poor
Basement	☐	☐	☐
Garage	☐	☐	☐

COMMUNITY

	Good	Average	Poor
Immediate Neighborhood	☐	☐	☐
Close to Employment	☐	☐	☐
Close to Shopping	☐	☐	☐
Close to Transportation	☐	☐	☐
Close to Schools / Daycare	☐	☐	☐
Close to Places of Worship	☐	☐	☐
Near Recreational Facilities	☐	☐	☐
Close to Airport	☐	☐	☐
Near Police and Fire Department	☐	☐	☐

Address _____ Price _____

Bedrooms _____ Bathrooms _____ Sq.Ft. _____

Lot Size: _____ Year Built _____ School District _____

Annual Tax _____

EXTERIOR

	Good	Average	Poor
View/Yard/Landscaping	☐	☐	☐
Trees	☐	☐	☐
Lawn (Front)	☐	☐	☐
Lawn (Back)	☐	☐	☐
Fences (condition)	☐	☐	☐
Landscaping (condition)	☐	☐	☐
Irrigation / Sprinkler	☐	☐	☐
	☐	☐	☐
House Type	☐	☐	☐
Exterior Siding	☐	☐	☐
Deck / Patio / Porch	☐	☐	☐
Garage	☐	☐	☐
Window / Doors	☐	☐	☐
Roof / Gutters	☐	☐	☐
Fencing	☐	☐	☐

HOME SYSTEMS

	Good	Average	Poor
Electrical	☐	☐	☐
Air Conditioning / Fans	☐	☐	☐
Heating	☐	☐	☐
Security	☐	☐	☐
Plumbing	☐	☐	☐
Intercom	☐	☐	☐

FEATURES

	Good	Average	Poor
Home Warranty	☐	☐	☐
Energy Saving Features	☐	☐	☐

INTERIOR

	Good	Average	Poor
Walls / Trim / Ceilings	☐	☐	☐
Flooring	☐	☐	☐
Stairs	☐	☐	☐
Storage	☐	☐	☐
Living Room	☐	☐	☐
Family Room	☐	☐	☐
Dining Room	☐	☐	☐

	Good	Average	Poor
Master Bedroom	☐	☐	☐
Bedroom 2	☐	☐	☐
Bedroom 3	☐	☐	☐
Bedroom 4	☐	☐	☐
Master Bathroom	☐	☐	☐
Bathroom 2	☐	☐	☐
Bathroom 3	☐	☐	☐
Bonus / Game Room	☐	☐	☐

	Good	Average	Poor
Kitchen	☐	☐	☐
Cabinets	☐	☐	☐
Countertop	☐	☐	☐
Counter Space	☐	☐	☐
Flooring	☐	☐	☐
Oven / Stove	☐	☐	☐
Microwave	☐	☐	☐
Layout	☐	☐	☐
Light Fixtures	☐	☐	☐
Backsplash	☐	☐	☐
Pantry	☐	☐	☐
Appliances	☐	☐	☐
Island	☐	☐	☐

	Good	Average	Poor
Basement	☐	☐	☐
Garage	☐	☐	☐

COMMUNITY

	Good	Average	Poor
Immediate Neighborhood	☐	☐	☐
Close to Employment	☐	☐	☐
Close to Shopping	☐	☐	☐
Close to Transportation	☐	☐	☐
Close to Schools / Daycare	☐	☐	☐
Close to Places of Worship	☐	☐	☐
Near Recreational Facilities	☐	☐	☐
Close to Airport	☐	☐	☐
Near Police and Fire Department	☐	☐	☐

Address _____ Price _____

Bedrooms _____ Bathrooms _____ Sq.Ft. _____

Lot Size: _____ Year Built _____ School District _____

Annual Tax _____

EXTERIOR

	Good	Average	Poor
View/Yard/Landscaping	☐	☐	☐
Trees	☐	☐	☐
Lawn (Front)	☐	☐	☐
Lawn (Back)	☐	☐	☐
Fences (condition)	☐	☐	☐
Landscaping (condition)	☐	☐	☐
Irrigation / Sprinkler	☐	☐	☐
	☐	☐	☐
House Type	☐	☐	☐
Exterior Siding	☐	☐	☐
Deck / Patio / Porch	☐	☐	☐
Garage	☐	☐	☐
Window / Doors	☐	☐	☐
Roof / Gutters	☐	☐	☐
Fencing	☐	☐	☐

HOME SYSTEMS

	Good	Average	Poor
Electrical	☐	☐	☐
Air Conditioning / Fans	☐	☐	☐
Heating	☐	☐	☐
Security	☐	☐	☐
Plumbing	☐	☐	☐
Intercom	☐	☐	☐

FEATURES

	Good	Average	Poor
Home Warranty	☐	☐	☐
Energy Saving Features	☐	☐	☐

INTERIOR

	Good	Average	Poor
Walls / Trim / Ceilings	☐	☐	☐
Flooring	☐	☐	☐
Stairs	☐	☐	☐
Storage	☐	☐	☐
Living Room	☐	☐	☐
Family Room	☐	☐	☐
Dining Room	☐	☐	☐

	Good	Average	Poor
Master Bedroom	☐	☐	☐
Bedroom 2	☐	☐	☐
Bedroom 3	☐	☐	☐
Bedroom 4	☐	☐	☐
Master Bathroom	☐	☐	☐
Bathroom 2	☐	☐	☐
Bathroom 3	☐	☐	☐
Bonus / Game Room	☐	☐	☐

	Good	Average	Poor
Kitchen	☐	☐	☐
Cabinets	☐	☐	☐
Countertop	☐	☐	☐
Counter Space	☐	☐	☐
Flooring	☐	☐	☐
Oven / Stove	☐	☐	☐
Microwave	☐	☐	☐
Layout	☐	☐	☐
Light Fixtures	☐	☐	☐
Backsplash	☐	☐	☐
Pantry	☐	☐	☐
Appliances	☐	☐	☐
Island	☐	☐	☐

	Good	Average	Poor
Basement	☐	☐	☐
Garage	☐	☐	☐

COMMUNITY

	Good	Average	Poor
Immediate Neighborhood	☐	☐	☐
Close to Employment	☐	☐	☐
Close to Shopping	☐	☐	☐
Close to Transportation	☐	☐	☐
Close to Schools / Daycare	☐	☐	☐
Close to Places of Worship	☐	☐	☐
Near Recreational Facilities	☐	☐	☐
Close to Airport	☐	☐	☐
Near Police and Fire Department	☐	☐	☐

Address _____ Price _____

Bedrooms _____ Bathrooms _____ Sq.Ft. _____

Lot Size: _____ Year Built _____ School District _____

Annual Tax _____

EXTERIOR

	Good	Average	Poor
View/Yard/Landscaping	☐	☐	☐
Trees	☐	☐	☐
Lawn (Front)	☐	☐	☐
Lawn (Back)	☐	☐	☐
Fences (condition)	☐	☐	☐
Landscaping (condition)	☐	☐	☐
Irrigation / Sprinkler	☐	☐	☐
	☐	☐	☐
House Type	☐	☐	☐
Exterior Siding	☐	☐	☐
Deck / Patio / Porch	☐	☐	☐
Garage	☐	☐	☐
Window / Doors	☐	☐	☐
Roof / Gutters	☐	☐	☐
Fencing	☐	☐	☐

HOME SYSTEMS

	Good	Average	Poor
Electrical	☐	☐	☐
Air Conditioning / Fans	☐	☐	☐
Heating	☐	☐	☐
Security	☐	☐	☐
Plumbing	☐	☐	☐
Intercom	☐	☐	☐

FEATURES

	Good	Average	Poor
Home Warranty	☐	☐	☐
Energy Saving Features	☐	☐	☐

INTERIOR

	Good	Average	Poor
Walls / Trim / Ceilings	☐	☐	☐
Flooring	☐	☐	☐
Stairs	☐	☐	☐
Storage	☐	☐	☐
Living Room	☐	☐	☐
Family Room	☐	☐	☐
Dining Room	☐	☐	☐

	Good	Average	Poor
Master Bedroom	☐	☐	☐
Bedroom 2	☐	☐	☐
Bedroom 3	☐	☐	☐
Bedroom 4	☐	☐	☐
Master Bathroom	☐	☐	☐
Bathroom 2	☐	☐	☐
Bathroom 3	☐	☐	☐
Bonus / Game Room	☐	☐	☐

	Good	Average	Poor
Kitchen	☐	☐	☐
Cabinets	☐	☐	☐
Countertop	☐	☐	☐
Counter Space	☐	☐	☐
Flooring	☐	☐	☐
Oven / Stove	☐	☐	☐
Microwave	☐	☐	☐
Layout	☐	☐	☐
Light Fixtures	☐	☐	☐
Backsplash	☐	☐	☐
Pantry	☐	☐	☐
Appliances	☐	☐	☐
Island	☐	☐	☐

	Good	Average	Poor
Basement	☐	☐	☐
Garage	☐	☐	☐

COMMUNITY

	Good	Average	Poor
Immediate Neighborhood	☐	☐	☐
Close to Employment	☐	☐	☐
Close to Shopping	☐	☐	☐
Close to Transportation	☐	☐	☐
Close to Schools / Daycare	☐	☐	☐
Close to Places of Worship	☐	☐	☐
Near Recreational Facilities	☐	☐	☐
Close to Airport	☐	☐	☐
Near Police and Fire Department	☐	☐	☐

Address _____ Price _____

Bedrooms _____ Bathrooms _____ Sq.Ft. _____

Lot Size: _____ Year Built _____ School District _____

Annual Tax _____

EXTERIOR

	Good	Average	Poor
View/Yard/Landscaping	☐	☐	☐
Trees	☐	☐	☐
Lawn (Front)	☐	☐	☐
Lawn (Back)	☐	☐	☐
Fences (condition)	☐	☐	☐
Landscaping (condition)	☐	☐	☐
Irrigation / Sprinkler	☐	☐	☐
	☐	☐	☐
House Type	☐	☐	☐
Exterior Siding	☐	☐	☐
Deck / Patio / Porch	☐	☐	☐
Garage	☐	☐	☐
Window / Doors	☐	☐	☐
Roof / Gutters	☐	☐	☐
Fencing	☐	☐	☐

HOME SYSTEMS

	Good	Average	Poor
Electrical	☐	☐	☐
Air Conditioning / Fans	☐	☐	☐
Heating	☐	☐	☐
Security	☐	☐	☐
Plumbing	☐	☐	☐
Intercom	☐	☐	☐

FEATURES

	Good	Average	Poor
Home Warranty	☐	☐	☐
Energy Saving Features	☐	☐	☐

INTERIOR

	Good	Average	Poor
Walls / Trim / Ceilings	☐	☐	☐
Flooring	☐	☐	☐
Stairs	☐	☐	☐
Storage	☐	☐	☐
Living Room	☐	☐	☐
Family Room	☐	☐	☐
Dining Room	☐	☐	☐

	Good	Average	Poor
Master Bedroom	☐	☐	☐
Bedroom 2	☐	☐	☐
Bedroom 3	☐	☐	☐
Bedroom 4	☐	☐	☐
Master Bathroom	☐	☐	☐
Bathroom 2	☐	☐	☐
Bathroom 3	☐	☐	☐
Bonus / Game Room	☐	☐	☐

	Good	Average	Poor
Kitchen			
Cabinets	☐	☐	☐
Countertop	☐	☐	☐
Counter Space	☐	☐	☐
Flooring	☐	☐	☐
Oven / Stove	☐	☐	☐
Microwave	☐	☐	☐
Layout	☐	☐	☐
Light Fixtures	☐	☐	☐
Backsplash	☐	☐	☐
Pantry	☐	☐	☐
Appliances	☐	☐	☐
Island	☐	☐	☐

	Good	Average	Poor
Basement	☐	☐	☐
Garage	☐	☐	☐

COMMUNITY

	Good	Average	Poor
Immediate Neighborhood	☐	☐	☐
Close to Employment	☐	☐	☐
Close to Shopping	☐	☐	☐
Close to Transportation	☐	☐	☐
Close to Schools / Daycare	☐	☐	☐
Close to Places of Worship	☐	☐	☐
Near Recreational Facilities	☐	☐	☐
Close to Airport	☐	☐	☐
Near Police and Fire Department	☐	☐	☐

Address _____ Price _____

Bedrooms _____ Bathrooms _____ Sq.Ft. _____

Lot Size: _____ Year Built _____ School District _____

Annual Tax _____

EXTERIOR

	Good	Average	Poor
View/Yard/Landscaping	☐	☐	☐
Trees	☐	☐	☐
Lawn (Front)	☐	☐	☐
Lawn (Back)	☐	☐	☐
Fences (condition)	☐	☐	☐
Landscaping (condition)	☐	☐	☐
Irrigation / Sprinkler	☐	☐	☐
	☐	☐	☐
House Type	☐	☐	☐
Exterior Siding	☐	☐	☐
Deck / Patio / Porch	☐	☐	☐
Garage	☐	☐	☐
Window / Doors	☐	☐	☐
Roof / Gutters	☐	☐	☐
Fencing	☐	☐	☐

HOME SYSTEMS

	Good	Average	Poor
Electrical	☐	☐	☐
Air Conditioning / Fans	☐	☐	☐
Heating	☐	☐	☐
Security	☐	☐	☐
Plumbing	☐	☐	☐
Intercom	☐	☐	☐

FEATURES

	Good	Average	Poor
Home Warranty	☐	☐	☐
Energy Saving Features	☐	☐	☐

INTERIOR

	Good	Average	Poor
Walls / Trim / Ceilings	☐	☐	☐
Flooring	☐	☐	☐
Stairs	☐	☐	☐
Storage	☐	☐	☐
Living Room	☐	☐	☐
Family Room	☐	☐	☐
Dining Room	☐	☐	☐

	Good	Average	Poor
Master Bedroom	☐	☐	☐
Bedroom 2	☐	☐	☐
Bedroom 3	☐	☐	☐
Bedroom 4	☐	☐	☐
Master Bathroom	☐	☐	☐
Bathroom 2	☐	☐	☐
Bathroom 3	☐	☐	☐
Bonus / Game Room	☐	☐	☐

	Good	Average	Poor
Kitchen			
Cabinets	☐	☐	☐
Countertop	☐	☐	☐
Counter Space	☐	☐	☐
Flooring	☐	☐	☐
Oven / Stove	☐	☐	☐
Microwave	☐	☐	☐
Layout	☐	☐	☐
Light Fixtures	☐	☐	☐
Backsplash	☐	☐	☐
Pantry	☐	☐	☐
Appliances	☐	☐	☐
Island	☐	☐	☐

	Good	Average	Poor
Basement	☐	☐	☐
Garage	☐	☐	☐

COMMUNITY

	Good	Average	Poor
Immediate Neighborhood	☐	☐	☐
Close to Employment	☐	☐	☐
Close to Shopping	☐	☐	☐
Close to Transportation	☐	☐	☐
Close to Schools / Daycare	☐	☐	☐
Close to Places of Worship	☐	☐	☐
Near Recreational Facilities	☐	☐	☐
Close to Airport	☐	☐	☐
Near Police and Fire Department	☐	☐	☐

Address _____ Price _____

Bedrooms _____ Bathrooms _____ Sq.Ft. _____

Lot Size: _____ Year Built _____ School District _____

Annual Tax _____

EXTERIOR

	Good	Average	Poor
View/Yard/Landscaping	☐	☐	☐
Trees	☐	☐	☐
Lawn (Front)	☐	☐	☐
Lawn (Back)	☐	☐	☐
Fences (condition)	☐	☐	☐
Landscaping (condition)	☐	☐	☐
Irrigation / Sprinkler	☐	☐	☐
	☐	☐	☐
House Type	☐	☐	☐
Exterior Siding	☐	☐	☐
Deck / Patio / Porch	☐	☐	☐
Garage	☐	☐	☐
Window / Doors	☐	☐	☐
Roof / Gutters	☐	☐	☐
Fencing	☐	☐	☐

HOME SYSTEMS

	Good	Average	Poor
Electrical	☐	☐	☐
Air Conditioning / Fans	☐	☐	☐
Heating	☐	☐	☐
Security	☐	☐	☐
Plumbing	☐	☐	☐
Intercom	☐	☐	☐

FEATURES

	Good	Average	Poor
Home Warranty	☐	☐	☐
Energy Saving Features	☐	☐	☐

INTERIOR

	Good	Average	Poor
Walls / Trim / Ceilings	☐	☐	☐
Flooring	☐	☐	☐
Stairs	☐	☐	☐
Storage	☐	☐	☐
Living Room	☐	☐	☐
Family Room	☐	☐	☐
Dining Room	☐	☐	☐

	Good	Average	Poor
Master Bedroom	☐	☐	☐
Bedroom 2	☐	☐	☐
Bedroom 3	☐	☐	☐
Bedroom 4	☐	☐	☐
Master Bathroom	☐	☐	☐
Bathroom 2	☐	☐	☐
Bathroom 3	☐	☐	☐
Bonus / Game Room	☐	☐	☐

	Good	Average	Poor
Kitchen			
Cabinets	☐	☐	☐
Countertop	☐	☐	☐
Counter Space	☐	☐	☐
Flooring	☐	☐	☐
Oven / Stove	☐	☐	☐
Microwave	☐	☐	☐
Layout	☐	☐	☐
Light Fixtures	☐	☐	☐
Backsplash	☐	☐	☐
Pantry	☐	☐	☐
Appliances	☐	☐	☐
Island	☐	☐	☐

	Good	Average	Poor
Basement	☐	☐	☐
Garage	☐	☐	☐

COMMUNITY

	Good	Average	Poor
Immediate Neighborhood	☐	☐	☐
Close to Employment	☐	☐	☐
Close to Shopping	☐	☐	☐
Close to Transportation	☐	☐	☐
Close to Schools / Daycare	☐	☐	☐
Close to Places of Worship	☐	☐	☐
Near Recreational Facilities	☐	☐	☐
Close to Airport	☐	☐	☐
Near Police and Fire Department	☐	☐	☐

Address _____ Price _____

Bedrooms _____ Bathrooms _____ Sq.Ft. _____

Lot Size: _____ Year Built _____ School District _____

Annual Tax _____

EXTERIOR

	Good	Average	Poor
View/Yard/Landscaping	☐	☐	☐
Trees	☐	☐	☐
Lawn (Front)	☐	☐	☐
Lawn (Back)	☐	☐	☐
Fences (condition)	☐	☐	☐
Landscaping (condition)	☐	☐	☐
Irrigation / Sprinkler	☐	☐	☐
	☐	☐	☐
House Type	☐	☐	☐
Exterior Siding	☐	☐	☐
Deck / Patio / Porch	☐	☐	☐
Garage	☐	☐	☐
Window / Doors	☐	☐	☐
Roof / Gutters	☐	☐	☐
Fencing	☐	☐	☐

HOME SYSTEMS

	Good	Average	Poor
Electrical	☐	☐	☐
Air Conditioning / Fans	☐	☐	☐
Heating	☐	☐	☐
Security	☐	☐	☐
Plumbing	☐	☐	☐
Intercom	☐	☐	☐

FEATURES

	Good	Average	Poor
Home Warranty	☐	☐	☐
Energy Saving Features	☐	☐	☐

INTERIOR

	Good	Average	Poor
Walls / Trim / Ceilings	☐	☐	☐
Flooring	☐	☐	☐
Stairs	☐	☐	☐
Storage	☐	☐	☐
Living Room	☐	☐	☐
Family Room	☐	☐	☐
Dining Room	☐	☐	☐

	Good	Average	Poor
Master Bedroom	☐	☐	☐
Bedroom 2	☐	☐	☐
Bedroom 3	☐	☐	☐
Bedroom 4	☐	☐	☐
Master Bathroom	☐	☐	☐
Bathroom 2	☐	☐	☐
Bathroom 3	☐	☐	☐
Bonus / Game Room	☐	☐	☐

	Good	Average	Poor
Kitchen	☐	☐	☐
Cabinets	☐	☐	☐
Countertop	☐	☐	☐
Counter Space	☐	☐	☐
Flooring	☐	☐	☐
Oven / Stove	☐	☐	☐
Microwave	☐	☐	☐
Layout	☐	☐	☐
Light Fixtures	☐	☐	☐
Backsplash	☐	☐	☐
Pantry	☐	☐	☐
Appliances	☐	☐	☐
Island	☐	☐	☐

	Good	Average	Poor
Basement	☐	☐	☐
Garage	☐	☐	☐

COMMUNITY

	Good	Average	Poor
Immediate Neighborhood	☐	☐	☐
Close to Employment	☐	☐	☐
Close to Shopping	☐	☐	☐
Close to Transportation	☐	☐	☐
Close to Schools / Daycare	☐	☐	☐
Close to Places of Worship	☐	☐	☐
Near Recreational Facilities	☐	☐	☐
Close to Airport	☐	☐	☐
Near Police and Fire Department	☐	☐	☐

Address _____ Price _____

Bedrooms _____ Bathrooms _____ Sq.Ft. _____

Lot Size: _____ Year Built _____ School District _____

Annual Tax _____

EXTERIOR

	Good	Average	Poor
View/Yard/Landscaping	☐	☐	☐
Trees	☐	☐	☐
Lawn (Front)	☐	☐	☐
Lawn (Back)	☐	☐	☐
Fences (condition)	☐	☐	☐
Landscaping (condition)	☐	☐	☐
Irrigation / Sprinkler	☐	☐	☐
	☐	☐	☐
House Type	☐	☐	☐
Exterior Siding	☐	☐	☐
Deck / Patio / Porch	☐	☐	☐
Garage	☐	☐	☐
Window / Doors	☐	☐	☐
Roof / Gutters	☐	☐	☐
Fencing	☐	☐	☐

HOME SYSTEMS

	Good	Average	Poor
Electrical	☐	☐	☐
Air Conditioning / Fans	☐	☐	☐
Heating	☐	☐	☐
Security	☐	☐	☐
Plumbing	☐	☐	☐
Intercom	☐	☐	☐

FEATURES

	Good	Average	Poor
Home Warranty	☐	☐	☐
Energy Saving Features	☐	☐	☐

INTERIOR

	Good	Average	Poor
Walls / Trim / Ceilings	☐	☐	☐
Flooring	☐	☐	☐
Stairs	☐	☐	☐
Storage	☐	☐	☐
Living Room	☐	☐	☐
Family Room	☐	☐	☐
Dining Room	☐	☐	☐

	Good	Average	Poor
Master Bedroom	☐	☐	☐
Bedroom 2	☐	☐	☐
Bedroom 3	☐	☐	☐
Bedroom 4	☐	☐	☐
Master Bathroom	☐	☐	☐
Bathroom 2	☐	☐	☐
Bathroom 3	☐	☐	☐
Bonus / Game Room	☐	☐	☐

	Good	Average	Poor
Kitchen			
Cabinets	☐	☐	☐
Countertop	☐	☐	☐
Counter Space	☐	☐	☐
Flooring	☐	☐	☐
Oven / Stove	☐	☐	☐
Microwave	☐	☐	☐
Layout	☐	☐	☐
Light Fixtures	☐	☐	☐
Backsplash	☐	☐	☐
Pantry	☐	☐	☐
Appliances	☐	☐	☐
Island	☐	☐	☐

	Good	Average	Poor
Basement	☐	☐	☐
Garage	☐	☐	☐

COMMUNITY

	Good	Average	Poor
Immediate Neighborhood	☐	☐	☐
Close to Employment	☐	☐	☐
Close to Shopping	☐	☐	☐
Close to Transportation	☐	☐	☐
Close to Schools / Daycare	☐	☐	☐
Close to Places of Worship	☐	☐	☐
Near Recreational Facilities	☐	☐	☐
Close to Airport	☐	☐	☐
Near Police and Fire Department	☐	☐	☐

Address _____ Price _____

Bedrooms _____ Bathrooms _____ Sq.Ft. _____

Lot Size: _____ Year Built _____ School District _____

Annual Tax _____

EXTERIOR

	Good	Average	Poor
View/Yard/Landscaping	☐	☐	☐
Trees	☐	☐	☐
Lawn (Front)	☐	☐	☐
Lawn (Back)	☐	☐	☐
Fences (condition)	☐	☐	☐
Landscaping (condition)	☐	☐	☐
Irrigation / Sprinkler	☐	☐	☐
	☐	☐	☐
House Type	☐	☐	☐
Exterior Siding	☐	☐	☐
Deck / Patio / Porch	☐	☐	☐
Garage	☐	☐	☐
Window / Doors	☐	☐	☐
Roof / Gutters	☐	☐	☐
Fencing	☐	☐	☐

HOME SYSTEMS

	Good	Average	Poor
Electrical	☐	☐	☐
Air Conditioning / Fans	☐	☐	☐
Heating	☐	☐	☐
Security	☐	☐	☐
Plumbing	☐	☐	☐
Intercom	☐	☐	☐

FEATURES

	Good	Average	Poor
Home Warranty	☐	☐	☐
Energy Saving Features	☐	☐	☐

INTERIOR

	Good	Average	Poor
Walls / Trim / Ceilings	☐	☐	☐
Flooring	☐	☐	☐
Stairs	☐	☐	☐
Storage	☐	☐	☐
Living Room	☐	☐	☐
Family Room	☐	☐	☐
Dining Room	☐	☐	☐

	Good	Average	Poor
Master Bedroom	☐	☐	☐
Bedroom 2	☐	☐	☐
Bedroom 3	☐	☐	☐
Bedroom 4	☐	☐	☐
Master Bathroom	☐	☐	☐
Bathroom 2	☐	☐	☐
Bathroom 3	☐	☐	☐
Bonus / Game Room	☐	☐	☐

	Good	Average	Poor
Kitchen			
Cabinets	☐	☐	☐
Countertop	☐	☐	☐
Counter Space	☐	☐	☐
Flooring	☐	☐	☐
Oven / Stove	☐	☐	☐
Microwave	☐	☐	☐
Layout	☐	☐	☐
Light Fixtures	☐	☐	☐
Backsplash	☐	☐	☐
Pantry	☐	☐	☐
Appliances	☐	☐	☐
Island	☐	☐	☐

	Good	Average	Poor
Basement	☐	☐	☐
Garage	☐	☐	☐

COMMUNITY

	Good	Average	Poor
Immediate Neighborhood	☐	☐	☐
Close to Employment	☐	☐	☐
Close to Shopping	☐	☐	☐
Close to Transportation	☐	☐	☐
Close to Schools / Daycare	☐	☐	☐
Close to Places of Worship	☐	☐	☐
Near Recreational Facilities	☐	☐	☐
Close to Airport	☐	☐	☐
Near Police and Fire Department	☐	☐	☐

Address _____ Price _____

Bedrooms _____ Bathrooms _____ Sq.Ft. _____

Lot Size: _____ Year Built _____ School District _____

Annual Tax _____

EXTERIOR

	Good	Average	Poor
View/Yard/Landscaping	☐	☐	☐
Trees	☐	☐	☐
Lawn (Front)	☐	☐	☐
Lawn (Back)	☐	☐	☐
Fences (condition)	☐	☐	☐
Landscaping (condition)	☐	☐	☐
Irrigation / Sprinkler	☐	☐	☐
	☐	☐	☐
House Type	☐	☐	☐
Exterior Siding	☐	☐	☐
Deck / Patio / Porch	☐	☐	☐
Garage	☐	☐	☐
Window / Doors	☐	☐	☐
Roof / Gutters	☐	☐	☐
Fencing	☐	☐	☐

HOME SYSTEMS

	Good	Average	Poor
Electrical	☐	☐	☐
Air Conditioning / Fans	☐	☐	☐
Heating	☐	☐	☐
Security	☐	☐	☐
Plumbing	☐	☐	☐
Intercom	☐	☐	☐

FEATURES

	Good	Average	Poor
Home Warranty	☐	☐	☐
Energy Saving Features	☐	☐	☐

INTERIOR

	Good	Average	Poor
Walls / Trim / Ceilings	☐	☐	☐
Flooring	☐	☐	☐
Stairs	☐	☐	☐
Storage	☐	☐	☐
Living Room	☐	☐	☐
Family Room	☐	☐	☐
Dining Room	☐	☐	☐

	Good	Average	Poor
Master Bedroom	☐	☐	☐
Bedroom 2	☐	☐	☐
Bedroom 3	☐	☐	☐
Bedroom 4	☐	☐	☐
Master Bathroom	☐	☐	☐
Bathroom 2	☐	☐	☐
Bathroom 3	☐	☐	☐
Bonus / Game Room	☐	☐	☐

	Good	Average	Poor
Kitchen			
Cabinets	☐	☐	☐
Countertop	☐	☐	☐
Counter Space	☐	☐	☐
Flooring	☐	☐	☐
Oven / Stove	☐	☐	☐
Microwave	☐	☐	☐
Layout	☐	☐	☐
Light Fixtures	☐	☐	☐
Backsplash	☐	☐	☐
Pantry	☐	☐	☐
Appliances	☐	☐	☐
Island	☐	☐	☐

	Good	Average	Poor
Basement	☐	☐	☐
Garage	☐	☐	☐

COMMUNITY

	Good	Average	Poor
Immediate Neighborhood	☐	☐	☐
Close to Employment	☐	☐	☐
Close to Shopping	☐	☐	☐
Close to Transportation	☐	☐	☐
Close to Schools / Daycare	☐	☐	☐
Close to Places of Worship	☐	☐	☐
Near Recreational Facilities	☐	☐	☐
Close to Airport	☐	☐	☐
Near Police and Fire Department	☐	☐	☐

Address _____   Price _____

Bedrooms _____   Bathrooms _____   Sq.Ft. _____

Lot Size: _____   Year Built _____   School District _____

Annual Tax _____

EXTERIOR

	Good	Average	Poor
View/Yard/Landscaping	☐	☐	☐
Trees	☐	☐	☐
Lawn (Front)	☐	☐	☐
Lawn (Back)	☐	☐	☐
Fences (condition)	☐	☐	☐
Landscaping (condition)	☐	☐	☐
Irrigation / Sprinkler	☐	☐	☐
	☐	☐	☐
House Type	☐	☐	☐
Exterior Siding	☐	☐	☐
Deck / Patio / Porch	☐	☐	☐
Garage	☐	☐	☐
Window / Doors	☐	☐	☐
Roof / Gutters	☐	☐	☐
Fencing	☐	☐	☐

HOME SYSTEMS

	Good	Average	Poor
Electrical	☐	☐	☐
Air Conditioning / Fans	☐	☐	☐
Heating	☐	☐	☐
Security	☐	☐	☐
Plumbing	☐	☐	☐
Intercom	☐	☐	☐

FEATURES

	Good	Average	Poor
Home Warranty	☐	☐	☐
Energy Saving Features	☐	☐	☐

INTERIOR

	Good	Average	Poor
Walls / Trim / Ceilings	☐	☐	☐
Flooring	☐	☐	☐
Stairs	☐	☐	☐
Storage	☐	☐	☐
Living Room	☐	☐	☐
Family Room	☐	☐	☐
Dining Room	☐	☐	☐

	Good	Average	Poor
Master Bedroom	☐	☐	☐
Bedroom 2	☐	☐	☐
Bedroom 3	☐	☐	☐
Bedroom 4	☐	☐	☐
Master Bathroom	☐	☐	☐
Bathroom 2	☐	☐	☐
Bathroom 3	☐	☐	☐
Bonus / Game Room	☐	☐	☐

	Good	Average	Poor
Kitchen			
Cabinets	☐	☐	☐
Countertop	☐	☐	☐
Counter Space	☐	☐	☐
Flooring	☐	☐	☐
Oven / Stove	☐	☐	☐
Microwave	☐	☐	☐
Layout	☐	☐	☐
Light Fixtures	☐	☐	☐
Backsplash	☐	☐	☐
Pantry	☐	☐	☐
Appliances	☐	☐	☐
Island	☐	☐	☐

	Good	Average	Poor
Basement	☐	☐	☐
Garage	☐	☐	☐

COMMUNITY

	Good	Average	Poor
Immediate Neighborhood	☐	☐	☐
Close to Employment	☐	☐	☐
Close to Shopping	☐	☐	☐
Close to Transportation	☐	☐	☐
Close to Schools / Daycare	☐	☐	☐
Close to Places of Worship	☐	☐	☐
Near Recreational Facilities	☐	☐	☐
Close to Airport	☐	☐	☐
Near Police and Fire Department	☐	☐	☐

Address _____ Price _____

Bedrooms _____ Bathrooms _____ Sq.Ft. _____

Lot Size: _____ Year Built _____ School District _____

Annual Tax _____

EXTERIOR

	Good	Average	Poor
View/Yard/Landscaping	☐	☐	☐
Trees	☐	☐	☐
Lawn (Front)	☐	☐	☐
Lawn (Back)	☐	☐	☐
Fences (condition)	☐	☐	☐
Landscaping (condition)	☐	☐	☐
Irrigation / Sprinkler	☐	☐	☐
	☐	☐	☐
House Type	☐	☐	☐
Exterior Siding	☐	☐	☐
Deck / Patio / Porch	☐	☐	☐
Garage	☐	☐	☐
Window / Doors	☐	☐	☐
Roof / Gutters	☐	☐	☐
Fencing	☐	☐	☐

HOME SYSTEMS

	Good	Average	Poor
Electrical	☐	☐	☐
Air Conditioning / Fans	☐	☐	☐
Heating	☐	☐	☐
Security	☐	☐	☐
Plumbing	☐	☐	☐
Intercom	☐	☐	☐

FEATURES

	Good	Average	Poor
Home Warranty	☐	☐	☐
Energy Saving Features	☐	☐	☐

INTERIOR

	Good	Average	Poor
Walls / Trim / Ceilings	☐	☐	☐
Flooring	☐	☐	☐
Stairs	☐	☐	☐
Storage	☐	☐	☐
Living Room	☐	☐	☐
Family Room	☐	☐	☐
Dining Room	☐	☐	☐

	Good	Average	Poor
Master Bedroom	☐	☐	☐
Bedroom 2	☐	☐	☐
Bedroom 3	☐	☐	☐
Bedroom 4	☐	☐	☐
Master Bathroom	☐	☐	☐
Bathroom 2	☐	☐	☐
Bathroom 3	☐	☐	☐
Bonus / Game Room	☐	☐	☐

	Good	Average	Poor
Kitchen	☐	☐	☐
Cabinets	☐	☐	☐
Countertop	☐	☐	☐
Counter Space	☐	☐	☐
Flooring	☐	☐	☐
Oven / Stove	☐	☐	☐
Microwave	☐	☐	☐
Layout	☐	☐	☐
Light Fixtures	☐	☐	☐
Backsplash	☐	☐	☐
Pantry	☐	☐	☐
Appliances	☐	☐	☐
Island	☐	☐	☐

	Good	Average	Poor
Basement	☐	☐	☐
Garage	☐	☐	☐

COMMUNITY

	Good	Average	Poor
Immediate Neighborhood	☐	☐	☐
Close to Employment	☐	☐	☐
Close to Shopping	☐	☐	☐
Close to Transportation	☐	☐	☐
Close to Schools / Daycare	☐	☐	☐
Close to Places of Worship	☐	☐	☐
Near Recreational Facilities	☐	☐	☐
Close to Airport	☐	☐	☐
Near Police and Fire Department	☐	☐	☐

Address _____ Price _____

Bedrooms _____ Bathrooms _____ Sq.Ft. _____

Lot Size: _____ Year Built _____ School District _____

Annual Tax _____

EXTERIOR

	Good	Average	Poor
View/Yard/Landscaping	☐	☐	☐
Trees	☐	☐	☐
Lawn (Front)	☐	☐	☐
Lawn (Back)	☐	☐	☐
Fences (condition)	☐	☐	☐
Landscaping (condition)	☐	☐	☐
Irrigation / Sprinkler	☐	☐	☐
	☐	☐	☐
House Type	☐	☐	☐
Exterior Siding	☐	☐	☐
Deck / Patio / Porch	☐	☐	☐
Garage	☐	☐	☐
Window / Doors	☐	☐	☐
Roof / Gutters	☐	☐	☐
Fencing	☐	☐	☐

HOME SYSTEMS

	Good	Average	Poor
Electrical	☐	☐	☐
Air Conditioning / Fans	☐	☐	☐
Heating	☐	☐	☐
Security	☐	☐	☐
Plumbing	☐	☐	☐
Intercom	☐	☐	☐

FEATURES

	Good	Average	Poor
Home Warranty	☐	☐	☐
Energy Saving Features	☐	☐	☐

INTERIOR

	Good	Average	Poor
Walls / Trim / Ceilings	☐	☐	☐
Flooring	☐	☐	☐
Stairs	☐	☐	☐
Storage	☐	☐	☐
Living Room	☐	☐	☐
Family Room	☐	☐	☐
Dining Room	☐	☐	☐

	Good	Average	Poor
Master Bedroom	☐	☐	☐
Bedroom 2	☐	☐	☐
Bedroom 3	☐	☐	☐
Bedroom 4	☐	☐	☐
Master Bathroom	☐	☐	☐
Bathroom 2	☐	☐	☐
Bathroom 3	☐	☐	☐
Bonus / Game Room	☐	☐	☐

	Good	Average	Poor
Kitchen	☐	☐	☐
Cabinets	☐	☐	☐
Countertop	☐	☐	☐
Counter Space	☐	☐	☐
Flooring	☐	☐	☐
Oven / Stove	☐	☐	☐
Microwave	☐	☐	☐
Layout	☐	☐	☐
Light Fixtures	☐	☐	☐
Backsplash	☐	☐	☐
Pantry	☐	☐	☐
Appliances	☐	☐	☐
Island	☐	☐	☐

	Good	Average	Poor
Basement	☐	☐	☐
Garage	☐	☐	☐

COMMUNITY

	Good	Average	Poor
Immediate Neighborhood	☐	☐	☐
Close to Employment	☐	☐	☐
Close to Shopping	☐	☐	☐
Close to Transportation	☐	☐	☐
Close to Schools / Daycare	☐	☐	☐
Close to Places of Worship	☐	☐	☐
Near Recreational Facilities	☐	☐	☐
Close to Airport	☐	☐	☐
Near Police and Fire Department	☐	☐	☐

Address _____ Price _____

Bedrooms _____ Bathrooms _____ Sq.Ft. _____

Lot Size: _____ Year Built _____ School District _____

Annual Tax _____

EXTERIOR

	Good	Average	Poor
View/Yard/Landscaping	☐	☐	☐
Trees	☐	☐	☐
Lawn (Front)	☐	☐	☐
Lawn (Back)	☐	☐	☐
Fences (condition)	☐	☐	☐
Landscaping (condition)	☐	☐	☐
Irrigation / Sprinkler	☐	☐	☐
	☐	☐	☐
House Type	☐	☐	☐
Exterior Siding	☐	☐	☐
Deck / Patio / Porch	☐	☐	☐
Garage	☐	☐	☐
Window / Doors	☐	☐	☐
Roof / Gutters	☐	☐	☐
Fencing	☐	☐	☐

HOME SYSTEMS

	Good	Average	Poor
Electrical	☐	☐	☐
Air Conditioning / Fans	☐	☐	☐
Heating	☐	☐	☐
Security	☐	☐	☐
Plumbing	☐	☐	☐
Intercom	☐	☐	☐

FEATURES

	Good	Average	Poor
Home Warranty	☐	☐	☐
Energy Saving Features	☐	☐	☐

INTERIOR

	Good	Average	Poor
Walls / Trim / Ceilings	☐	☐	☐
Flooring	☐	☐	☐
Stairs	☐	☐	☐
Storage	☐	☐	☐
Living Room	☐	☐	☐
Family Room	☐	☐	☐
Dining Room	☐	☐	☐

	Good	Average	Poor
Master Bedroom	☐	☐	☐
Bedroom 2	☐	☐	☐
Bedroom 3	☐	☐	☐
Bedroom 4	☐	☐	☐
Master Bathroom	☐	☐	☐
Bathroom 2	☐	☐	☐
Bathroom 3	☐	☐	☐
Bonus / Game Room	☐	☐	☐

	Good	Average	Poor
Kitchen	☐	☐	☐
Cabinets	☐	☐	☐
Countertop	☐	☐	☐
Counter Space	☐	☐	☐
Flooring	☐	☐	☐
Oven / Stove	☐	☐	☐
Microwave	☐	☐	☐
Layout	☐	☐	☐
Light Fixtures	☐	☐	☐
Backsplash	☐	☐	☐
Pantry	☐	☐	☐
Appliances	☐	☐	☐
Island	☐	☐	☐

	Good	Average	Poor
Basement	☐	☐	☐
Garage	☐	☐	☐

COMMUNITY

	Good	Average	Poor
Immediate Neighborhood	☐	☐	☐
Close to Employment	☐	☐	☐
Close to Shopping	☐	☐	☐
Close to Transportation	☐	☐	☐
Close to Schools / Daycare	☐	☐	☐
Close to Places of Worship	☐	☐	☐
Near Recreational Facilities	☐	☐	☐
Close to Airport	☐	☐	☐
Near Police and Fire Department	☐	☐	☐

Address _____ Price _____

Bedrooms _____ Bathrooms _____ Sq.Ft. _____

Lot Size: _____ Year Built _____ School District _____

Annual Tax _____

EXTERIOR

	Good	Average	Poor
View/Yard/Landscaping	☐	☐	☐
Trees	☐	☐	☐
Lawn (Front)	☐	☐	☐
Lawn (Back)	☐	☐	☐
Fences (condition)	☐	☐	☐
Landscaping (condition)	☐	☐	☐
Irrigation / Sprinkler	☐	☐	☐
	☐	☐	☐
House Type	☐	☐	☐
Exterior Siding	☐	☐	☐
Deck / Patio / Porch	☐	☐	☐
Garage	☐	☐	☐
Window / Doors	☐	☐	☐
Roof / Gutters	☐	☐	☐
Fencing	☐	☐	☐

HOME SYSTEMS

	Good	Average	Poor
Electrical	☐	☐	☐
Air Conditioning / Fans	☐	☐	☐
Heating	☐	☐	☐
Security	☐	☐	☐
Plumbing	☐	☐	☐
Intercom	☐	☐	☐

FEATURES

	Good	Average	Poor
Home Warranty	☐	☐	☐
Energy Saving Features	☐	☐	☐

INTERIOR

	Good	Average	Poor
Walls / Trim / Ceilings	☐	☐	☐
Flooring	☐	☐	☐
Stairs	☐	☐	☐
Storage	☐	☐	☐
Living Room	☐	☐	☐
Family Room	☐	☐	☐
Dining Room	☐	☐	☐

	Good	Average	Poor
Master Bedroom	☐	☐	☐
Bedroom 2	☐	☐	☐
Bedroom 3	☐	☐	☐
Bedroom 4	☐	☐	☐
Master Bathroom	☐	☐	☐
Bathroom 2	☐	☐	☐
Bathroom 3	☐	☐	☐
Bonus / Game Room	☐	☐	☐

	Good	Average	Poor
Kitchen			
Cabinets	☐	☐	☐
Countertop	☐	☐	☐
Counter Space	☐	☐	☐
Flooring	☐	☐	☐
Oven / Stove	☐	☐	☐
Microwave	☐	☐	☐
Layout	☐	☐	☐
Light Fixtures	☐	☐	☐
Backsplash	☐	☐	☐
Pantry	☐	☐	☐
Appliances	☐	☐	☐
Island	☐	☐	☐

	Good	Average	Poor
Basement	☐	☐	☐
Garage	☐	☐	☐

COMMUNITY

	Good	Average	Poor
Immediate Neighborhood	☐	☐	☐
Close to Employment	☐	☐	☐
Close to Shopping	☐	☐	☐
Close to Transportation	☐	☐	☐
Close to Schools / Daycare	☐	☐	☐
Close to Places of Worship	☐	☐	☐
Near Recreational Facilities	☐	☐	☐
Close to Airport	☐	☐	☐
Near Police and Fire Department	☐	☐	☐

Address _____ Price _____

Bedrooms _____ Bathrooms _____ Sq.Ft. _____

Lot Size: _____ Year Built _____ School District _____

Annual Tax _____

EXTERIOR

	Good	Average	Poor
View/Yard/Landscaping	☐	☐	☐
Trees	☐	☐	☐
Lawn (Front)	☐	☐	☐
Lawn (Back)	☐	☐	☐
Fences (condition)	☐	☐	☐
Landscaping (condition)	☐	☐	☐
Irrigation / Sprinkler	☐	☐	☐
	☐	☐	☐
House Type	☐	☐	☐
Exterior Siding	☐	☐	☐
Deck / Patio / Porch	☐	☐	☐
Garage	☐	☐	☐
Window / Doors	☐	☐	☐
Roof / Gutters	☐	☐	☐
Fencing	☐	☐	☐

HOME SYSTEMS

	Good	Average	Poor
Electrical	☐	☐	☐
Air Conditioning / Fans	☐	☐	☐
Heating	☐	☐	☐
Security	☐	☐	☐
Plumbing	☐	☐	☐
Intercom	☐	☐	☐

FEATURES

	Good	Average	Poor
Home Warranty	☐	☐	☐
Energy Saving Features	☐	☐	☐

INTERIOR

	Good	Average	Poor
Walls / Trim / Ceilings	☐	☐	☐
Flooring	☐	☐	☐
Stairs	☐	☐	☐
Storage	☐	☐	☐
Living Room	☐	☐	☐
Family Room	☐	☐	☐
Dining Room	☐	☐	☐

	Good	Average	Poor
Master Bedroom	☐	☐	☐
Bedroom 2	☐	☐	☐
Bedroom 3	☐	☐	☐
Bedroom 4	☐	☐	☐
Master Bathroom	☐	☐	☐
Bathroom 2	☐	☐	☐
Bathroom 3	☐	☐	☐
Bonus / Game Room	☐	☐	☐

	Good	Average	Poor
Kitchen	☐	☐	☐
Cabinets	☐	☐	☐
Countertop	☐	☐	☐
Counter Space	☐	☐	☐
Flooring	☐	☐	☐
Oven / Stove	☐	☐	☐
Microwave	☐	☐	☐
Layout	☐	☐	☐
Light Fixtures	☐	☐	☐
Backsplash	☐	☐	☐
Pantry	☐	☐	☐
Appliances	☐	☐	☐
Island	☐	☐	☐

	Good	Average	Poor
Basement	☐	☐	☐
Garage	☐	☐	☐

COMMUNITY

	Good	Average	Poor
Immediate Neighborhood	☐	☐	☐
Close to Employment	☐	☐	☐
Close to Shopping	☐	☐	☐
Close to Transportation	☐	☐	☐
Close to Schools / Daycare	☐	☐	☐
Close to Places of Worship	☐	☐	☐
Near Recreational Facilities	☐	☐	☐
Close to Airport	☐	☐	☐
Near Police and Fire Department	☐	☐	☐

Address _____ Price _____

Bedrooms _____ Bathrooms _____ Sq.Ft. _____

Lot Size: _____ Year Built _____ School District _____

Annual Tax _____

EXTERIOR

	Good	Average	Poor
View/Yard/Landscaping	☐	☐	☐
Trees	☐	☐	☐
Lawn (Front)	☐	☐	☐
Lawn (Back)	☐	☐	☐
Fences (condition)	☐	☐	☐
Landscaping (condition)	☐	☐	☐
Irrigation / Sprinkler	☐	☐	☐
	☐	☐	☐
House Type	☐	☐	☐
Exterior Siding	☐	☐	☐
Deck / Patio / Porch	☐	☐	☐
Garage	☐	☐	☐
Window / Doors	☐	☐	☐
Roof / Gutters	☐	☐	☐
Fencing	☐	☐	☐

HOME SYSTEMS

	Good	Average	Poor
Electrical	☐	☐	☐
Air Conditioning / Fans	☐	☐	☐
Heating	☐	☐	☐
Security	☐	☐	☐
Plumbing	☐	☐	☐
Intercom	☐	☐	☐

FEATURES

	Good	Average	Poor
Home Warranty	☐	☐	☐
Energy Saving Features	☐	☐	☐

INTERIOR

	Good	Average	Poor
Walls / Trim / Ceilings	☐	☐	☐
Flooring	☐	☐	☐
Stairs	☐	☐	☐
Storage	☐	☐	☐
Living Room	☐	☐	☐
Family Room	☐	☐	☐
Dining Room	☐	☐	☐

	Good	Average	Poor
Master Bedroom	☐	☐	☐
Bedroom 2	☐	☐	☐
Bedroom 3	☐	☐	☐
Bedroom 4	☐	☐	☐
Master Bathroom	☐	☐	☐
Bathroom 2	☐	☐	☐
Bathroom 3	☐	☐	☐
Bonus / Game Room	☐	☐	☐

	Good	Average	Poor
Kitchen			
Cabinets	☐	☐	☐
Countertop	☐	☐	☐
Counter Space	☐	☐	☐
Flooring	☐	☐	☐
Oven / Stove	☐	☐	☐
Microwave	☐	☐	☐
Layout	☐	☐	☐
Light Fixtures	☐	☐	☐
Backsplash	☐	☐	☐
Pantry	☐	☐	☐
Appliances	☐	☐	☐
Island	☐	☐	☐

	Good	Average	Poor
Basement	☐	☐	☐
Garage	☐	☐	☐

COMMUNITY

	Good	Average	Poor
Immediate Neighborhood	☐	☐	☐
Close to Employment	☐	☐	☐
Close to Shopping	☐	☐	☐
Close to Transportation	☐	☐	☐
Close to Schools / Daycare	☐	☐	☐
Close to Places of Worship	☐	☐	☐
Near Recreational Facilities	☐	☐	☐
Close to Airport	☐	☐	☐
Near Police and Fire Department	☐	☐	☐

Address _____ Price _____

Bedrooms _____ Bathrooms _____ Sq.Ft. _____

Lot Size: _____ Year Built _____ School District _____

Annual Tax _____

EXTERIOR

	Good	Average	Poor
View/Yard/Landscaping	☐	☐	☐
Trees	☐	☐	☐
Lawn (Front)	☐	☐	☐
Lawn (Back)	☐	☐	☐
Fences (condition)	☐	☐	☐
Landscaping (condition)	☐	☐	☐
Irrigation / Sprinkler	☐	☐	☐
	☐	☐	☐
House Type	☐	☐	☐
Exterior Siding	☐	☐	☐
Deck / Patio / Porch	☐	☐	☐
Garage	☐	☐	☐
Window / Doors	☐	☐	☐
Roof / Gutters	☐	☐	☐
Fencing	☐	☐	☐

HOME SYSTEMS

	Good	Average	Poor
Electrical	☐	☐	☐
Air Conditioning / Fans	☐	☐	☐
Heating	☐	☐	☐
Security	☐	☐	☐
Plumbing	☐	☐	☐
Intercom	☐	☐	☐

FEATURES

	Good	Average	Poor
Home Warranty	☐	☐	☐
Energy Saving Features	☐	☐	☐

INTERIOR

	Good	Average	Poor
Walls / Trim / Ceilings	☐	☐	☐
Flooring	☐	☐	☐
Stairs	☐	☐	☐
Storage	☐	☐	☐
Living Room	☐	☐	☐
Family Room	☐	☐	☐
Dining Room	☐	☐	☐

	Good	Average	Poor
Master Bedroom	☐	☐	☐
Bedroom 2	☐	☐	☐
Bedroom 3	☐	☐	☐
Bedroom 4	☐	☐	☐
Master Bathroom	☐	☐	☐
Bathroom 2	☐	☐	☐
Bathroom 3	☐	☐	☐
Bonus / Game Room	☐	☐	☐

	Good	Average	Poor
Kitchen			
Cabinets	☐	☐	☐
Countertop	☐	☐	☐
Counter Space	☐	☐	☐
Flooring	☐	☐	☐
Oven / Stove	☐	☐	☐
Microwave	☐	☐	☐
Layout	☐	☐	☐
Light Fixtures	☐	☐	☐
Backsplash	☐	☐	☐
Pantry	☐	☐	☐
Appliances	☐	☐	☐
Island	☐	☐	☐

	Good	Average	Poor
Basement	☐	☐	☐
Garage	☐	☐	☐

COMMUNITY

	Good	Average	Poor
Immediate Neighborhood	☐	☐	☐
Close to Employment	☐	☐	☐
Close to Shopping	☐	☐	☐
Close to Transportation	☐	☐	☐
Close to Schools / Daycare	☐	☐	☐
Close to Places of Worship	☐	☐	☐
Near Recreational Facilities	☐	☐	☐
Close to Airport	☐	☐	☐
Near Police and Fire Department	☐	☐	☐

Address _____ Price _____

Bedrooms _____ Bathrooms _____ Sq.Ft. _____

Lot Size: _____ Year Built _____ School District _____

Annual Tax _____

EXTERIOR

	Good	Average	Poor
View/Yard/Landscaping	☐	☐	☐
Trees	☐	☐	☐
Lawn (Front)	☐	☐	☐
Lawn (Back)	☐	☐	☐
Fences (condition)	☐	☐	☐
Landscaping (condition)	☐	☐	☐
Irrigation / Sprinkler	☐	☐	☐
	☐	☐	☐
House Type	☐	☐	☐
Exterior Siding	☐	☐	☐
Deck / Patio / Porch	☐	☐	☐
Garage	☐	☐	☐
Window / Doors	☐	☐	☐
Roof / Gutters	☐	☐	☐
Fencing	☐	☐	☐

HOME SYSTEMS

	Good	Average	Poor
Electrical	☐	☐	☐
Air Conditioning / Fans	☐	☐	☐
Heating	☐	☐	☐
Security	☐	☐	☐
Plumbing	☐	☐	☐
Intercom	☐	☐	☐

FEATURES

	Good	Average	Poor
Home Warranty	☐	☐	☐
Energy Saving Features	☐	☐	☐

INTERIOR

	Good	Average	Poor
Walls / Trim / Ceilings	☐	☐	☐
Flooring	☐	☐	☐
Stairs	☐	☐	☐
Storage	☐	☐	☐
Living Room	☐	☐	☐
Family Room	☐	☐	☐
Dining Room	☐	☐	☐

	Good	Average	Poor
Master Bedroom	☐	☐	☐
Bedroom 2	☐	☐	☐
Bedroom 3	☐	☐	☐
Bedroom 4	☐	☐	☐
Master Bathroom	☐	☐	☐
Bathroom 2	☐	☐	☐
Bathroom 3	☐	☐	☐
Bonus / Game Room	☐	☐	☐

	Good	Average	Poor
Kitchen	☐	☐	☐
Cabinets	☐	☐	☐
Countertop	☐	☐	☐
Counter Space	☐	☐	☐
Flooring	☐	☐	☐
Oven / Stove	☐	☐	☐
Microwave	☐	☐	☐
Layout	☐	☐	☐
Light Fixtures	☐	☐	☐
Backsplash	☐	☐	☐
Pantry	☐	☐	☐
Appliances	☐	☐	☐
Island	☐	☐	☐

	Good	Average	Poor
Basement	☐	☐	☐
Garage	☐	☐	☐

COMMUNITY

	Good	Average	Poor
Immediate Neighborhood	☐	☐	☐
Close to Employment	☐	☐	☐
Close to Shopping	☐	☐	☐
Close to Transportation	☐	☐	☐
Close to Schools / Daycare	☐	☐	☐
Close to Places of Worship	☐	☐	☐
Near Recreational Facilities	☐	☐	☐
Close to Airport	☐	☐	☐
Near Police and Fire Department	☐	☐	☐

Address _____ Price _____

Bedrooms _____ Bathrooms _____ Sq.Ft. _____

Lot Size: _____ Year Built _____ School District _____

Annual Tax _____

EXTERIOR

	Good	Average	Poor
View/Yard/Landscaping	☐	☐	☐
Trees	☐	☐	☐
Lawn (Front)	☐	☐	☐
Lawn (Back)	☐	☐	☐
Fences (condition)	☐	☐	☐
Landscaping (condition)	☐	☐	☐
Irrigation / Sprinkler	☐	☐	☐
	☐	☐	☐
House Type	☐	☐	☐
Exterior Siding	☐	☐	☐
Deck / Patio / Porch	☐	☐	☐
Garage	☐	☐	☐
Window / Doors	☐	☐	☐
Roof / Gutters	☐	☐	☐
Fencing	☐	☐	☐

HOME SYSTEMS

	Good	Average	Poor
Electrical	☐	☐	☐
Air Conditioning / Fans	☐	☐	☐
Heating	☐	☐	☐
Security	☐	☐	☐
Plumbing	☐	☐	☐
Intercom	☐	☐	☐

FEATURES

	Good	Average	Poor
Home Warranty	☐	☐	☐
Energy Saving Features	☐	☐	☐

INTERIOR

	Good	Average	Poor
Walls / Trim / Ceilings	☐	☐	☐
Flooring	☐	☐	☐
Stairs	☐	☐	☐
Storage	☐	☐	☐
Living Room	☐	☐	☐
Family Room	☐	☐	☐
Dining Room	☐	☐	☐

	Good	Average	Poor
Master Bedroom	☐	☐	☐
Bedroom 2	☐	☐	☐
Bedroom 3	☐	☐	☐
Bedroom 4	☐	☐	☐
Master Bathroom	☐	☐	☐
Bathroom 2	☐	☐	☐
Bathroom 3	☐	☐	☐
Bonus / Game Room	☐	☐	☐

	Good	Average	Poor
Kitchen	☐	☐	☐
Cabinets	☐	☐	☐
Countertop	☐	☐	☐
Counter Space	☐	☐	☐
Flooring	☐	☐	☐
Oven / Stove	☐	☐	☐
Microwave	☐	☐	☐
Layout	☐	☐	☐
Light Fixtures	☐	☐	☐
Backsplash	☐	☐	☐
Pantry	☐	☐	☐
Appliances	☐	☐	☐
Island	☐	☐	☐

	Good	Average	Poor
Basement	☐	☐	☐
Garage	☐	☐	☐

COMMUNITY

	Good	Average	Poor
Immediate Neighborhood	☐	☐	☐
Close to Employment	☐	☐	☐
Close to Shopping	☐	☐	☐
Close to Transportation	☐	☐	☐
Close to Schools / Daycare	☐	☐	☐
Close to Places of Worship	☐	☐	☐
Near Recreational Facilities	☐	☐	☐
Close to Airport	☐	☐	☐
Near Police and Fire Department	☐	☐	☐

Address _____ Price _____

Bedrooms _____ Bathrooms _____ Sq.Ft. _____

Lot Size: _____ Year Built _____ School District _____

Annual Tax _____

EXTERIOR

	Good	Average	Poor
View/Yard/Landscaping	☐	☐	☐
Trees	☐	☐	☐
Lawn (Front)	☐	☐	☐
Lawn (Back)	☐	☐	☐
Fences (condition)	☐	☐	☐
Landscaping (condition)	☐	☐	☐
Irrigation / Sprinkler	☐	☐	☐
	☐	☐	☐
House Type	☐	☐	☐
Exterior Siding	☐	☐	☐
Deck / Patio / Porch	☐	☐	☐
Garage	☐	☐	☐
Window / Doors	☐	☐	☐
Roof / Gutters	☐	☐	☐
Fencing	☐	☐	☐

HOME SYSTEMS

	Good	Average	Poor
Electrical	☐	☐	☐
Air Conditioning / Fans	☐	☐	☐
Heating	☐	☐	☐
Security	☐	☐	☐
Plumbing	☐	☐	☐
Intercom	☐	☐	☐

FEATURES

	Good	Average	Poor
Home Warranty	☐	☐	☐
Energy Saving Features	☐	☐	☐

INTERIOR

	Good	Average	Poor
Walls / Trim / Ceilings	☐	☐	☐
Flooring	☐	☐	☐
Stairs	☐	☐	☐
Storage	☐	☐	☐
Living Room	☐	☐	☐
Family Room	☐	☐	☐
Dining Room	☐	☐	☐

	Good	Average	Poor
Master Bedroom	☐	☐	☐
Bedroom 2	☐	☐	☐
Bedroom 3	☐	☐	☐
Bedroom 4	☐	☐	☐
Master Bathroom	☐	☐	☐
Bathroom 2	☐	☐	☐
Bathroom 3	☐	☐	☐
Bonus / Game Room	☐	☐	☐

	Good	Average	Poor
Kitchen			
Cabinets	☐	☐	☐
Countertop	☐	☐	☐
Counter Space	☐	☐	☐
Flooring	☐	☐	☐
Oven / Stove	☐	☐	☐
Microwave	☐	☐	☐
Layout	☐	☐	☐
Light Fixtures	☐	☐	☐
Backsplash	☐	☐	☐
Pantry	☐	☐	☐
Appliances	☐	☐	☐
Island	☐	☐	☐

	Good	Average	Poor
Basement	☐	☐	☐
Garage	☐	☐	☐

COMMUNITY

	Good	Average	Poor
Immediate Neighborhood	☐	☐	☐
Close to Employment	☐	☐	☐
Close to Shopping	☐	☐	☐
Close to Transportation	☐	☐	☐
Close to Schools / Daycare	☐	☐	☐
Close to Places of Worship	☐	☐	☐
Near Recreational Facilities	☐	☐	☐
Close to Airport	☐	☐	☐
Near Police and Fire Department	☐	☐	☐

Address _____ Price _____

Bedrooms _____ Bathrooms _____ Sq.Ft. _____

Lot Size: _____ Year Built _____ School District _____

Annual Tax _____

EXTERIOR

	Good	Average	Poor
View/Yard/Landscaping	☐	☐	☐
Trees	☐	☐	☐
Lawn (Front)	☐	☐	☐
Lawn (Back)	☐	☐	☐
Fences (condition)	☐	☐	☐
Landscaping (condition)	☐	☐	☐
Irrigation / Sprinkler	☐	☐	☐
	☐	☐	☐
House Type	☐	☐	☐
Exterior Siding	☐	☐	☐
Deck / Patio / Porch	☐	☐	☐
Garage	☐	☐	☐
Window / Doors	☐	☐	☐
Roof / Gutters	☐	☐	☐
Fencing	☐	☐	☐

HOME SYSTEMS

	Good	Average	Poor
Electrical	☐	☐	☐
Air Conditioning / Fans	☐	☐	☐
Heating	☐	☐	☐
Security	☐	☐	☐
Plumbing	☐	☐	☐
Intercom	☐	☐	☐

FEATURES

	Good	Average	Poor
Home Warranty	☐	☐	☐
Energy Saving Features	☐	☐	☐

INTERIOR

	Good	Average	Poor
Walls / Trim / Ceilings	☐	☐	☐
Flooring	☐	☐	☐
Stairs	☐	☐	☐
Storage	☐	☐	☐
Living Room	☐	☐	☐
Family Room	☐	☐	☐
Dining Room	☐	☐	☐

	Good	Average	Poor
Master Bedroom	☐	☐	☐
Bedroom 2	☐	☐	☐
Bedroom 3	☐	☐	☐
Bedroom 4	☐	☐	☐
Master Bathroom	☐	☐	☐
Bathroom 2	☐	☐	☐
Bathroom 3	☐	☐	☐
Bonus / Game Room	☐	☐	☐

	Good	Average	Poor
Kitchen	☐	☐	☐
Cabinets	☐	☐	☐
Countertop	☐	☐	☐
Counter Space	☐	☐	☐
Flooring	☐	☐	☐
Oven / Stove	☐	☐	☐
Microwave	☐	☐	☐
Layout	☐	☐	☐
Light Fixtures	☐	☐	☐
Backsplash	☐	☐	☐
Pantry	☐	☐	☐
Appliances	☐	☐	☐
Island	☐	☐	☐

	Good	Average	Poor
Basement	☐	☐	☐
Garage	☐	☐	☐

COMMUNITY

	Good	Average	Poor
Immediate Neighborhood	☐	☐	☐
Close to Employment	☐	☐	☐
Close to Shopping	☐	☐	☐
Close to Transportation	☐	☐	☐
Close to Schools / Daycare	☐	☐	☐
Close to Places of Worship	☐	☐	☐
Near Recreational Facilities	☐	☐	☐
Close to Airport	☐	☐	☐
Near Police and Fire Department	☐	☐	☐

Address _____ Price _____

Bedrooms _____ Bathrooms _____ Sq.Ft. _____

Lot Size: _____ Year Built _____ School District _____

Annual Tax _____

EXTERIOR

	Good	Average	Poor
View/Yard/Landscaping	☐	☐	☐
Trees	☐	☐	☐
Lawn (Front)	☐	☐	☐
Lawn (Back)	☐	☐	☐
Fences (condition)	☐	☐	☐
Landscaping (condition)	☐	☐	☐
Irrigation / Sprinkler	☐	☐	☐
	☐	☐	☐
House Type	☐	☐	☐
Exterior Siding	☐	☐	☐
Deck / Patio / Porch	☐	☐	☐
Garage	☐	☐	☐
Window / Doors	☐	☐	☐
Roof / Gutters	☐	☐	☐
Fencing	☐	☐	☐

HOME SYSTEMS

	Good	Average	Poor
Electrical	☐	☐	☐
Air Conditioning / Fans	☐	☐	☐
Heating	☐	☐	☐
Security	☐	☐	☐
Plumbing	☐	☐	☐
Intercom	☐	☐	☐

FEATURES

	Good	Average	Poor
Home Warranty	☐	☐	☐
Energy Saving Features	☐	☐	☐

INTERIOR

	Good	Average	Poor
Walls / Trim / Ceilings	☐	☐	☐
Flooring	☐	☐	☐
Stairs	☐	☐	☐
Storage	☐	☐	☐
Living Room	☐	☐	☐
Family Room	☐	☐	☐
Dining Room	☐	☐	☐

	Good	Average	Poor
Master Bedroom	☐	☐	☐
Bedroom 2	☐	☐	☐
Bedroom 3	☐	☐	☐
Bedroom 4	☐	☐	☐
Master Bathroom	☐	☐	☐
Bathroom 2	☐	☐	☐
Bathroom 3	☐	☐	☐
Bonus / Game Room	☐	☐	☐

	Good	Average	Poor
Kitchen			
Cabinets	☐	☐	☐
Countertop	☐	☐	☐
Counter Space	☐	☐	☐
Flooring	☐	☐	☐
Oven / Stove	☐	☐	☐
Microwave	☐	☐	☐
Layout	☐	☐	☐
Light Fixtures	☐	☐	☐
Backsplash	☐	☐	☐
Pantry	☐	☐	☐
Appliances	☐	☐	☐
Island	☐	☐	☐

	Good	Average	Poor
Basement	☐	☐	☐
Garage	☐	☐	☐

COMMUNITY

	Good	Average	Poor
Immediate Neighborhood	☐	☐	☐
Close to Employment	☐	☐	☐
Close to Shopping	☐	☐	☐
Close to Transportation	☐	☐	☐
Close to Schools / Daycare	☐	☐	☐
Close to Places of Worship	☐	☐	☐
Near Recreational Facilities	☐	☐	☐
Close to Airport	☐	☐	☐
Near Police and Fire Department	☐	☐	☐

Address _____ Price _____

Bedrooms _____ Bathrooms _____ Sq.Ft. _____

Lot Size: _____ Year Built _____ School District _____

Annual Tax _____

EXTERIOR

	Good	Average	Poor
View/Yard/Landscaping	☐	☐	☐
Trees	☐	☐	☐
Lawn (Front)	☐	☐	☐
Lawn (Back)	☐	☐	☐
Fences (condition)	☐	☐	☐
Landscaping (condition)	☐	☐	☐
Irrigation / Sprinkler	☐	☐	☐
House Type	☐	☐	☐
Exterior Siding	☐	☐	☐
Deck / Patio / Porch	☐	☐	☐
Garage	☐	☐	☐
Window / Doors	☐	☐	☐
Roof / Gutters	☐	☐	☐
Fencing	☐	☐	☐

HOME SYSTEMS

	Good	Average	Poor
Electrical	☐	☐	☐
Air Conditioning / Fans	☐	☐	☐
Heating	☐	☐	☐
Security	☐	☐	☐
Plumbing	☐	☐	☐
Intercom	☐	☐	☐

FEATURES

	Good	Average	Poor
Home Warranty	☐	☐	☐
Energy Saving Features	☐	☐	☐

INTERIOR

	Good	Average	Poor
Walls / Trim / Ceilings	☐	☐	☐
Flooring	☐	☐	☐
Stairs	☐	☐	☐
Storage	☐	☐	☐
Living Room	☐	☐	☐
Family Room	☐	☐	☐
Dining Room	☐	☐	☐

	Good	Average	Poor
Master Bedroom	☐	☐	☐
Bedroom 2	☐	☐	☐
Bedroom 3	☐	☐	☐
Bedroom 4	☐	☐	☐
Master Bathroom	☐	☐	☐
Bathroom 2	☐	☐	☐
Bathroom 3	☐	☐	☐
Bonus / Game Room	☐	☐	☐

	Good	Average	Poor
Kitchen			
Cabinets	☐	☐	☐
Countertop	☐	☐	☐
Counter Space	☐	☐	☐
Flooring	☐	☐	☐
Oven / Stove	☐	☐	☐
Microwave	☐	☐	☐
Layout	☐	☐	☐
Light Fixtures	☐	☐	☐
Backsplash	☐	☐	☐
Pantry	☐	☐	☐
Appliances	☐	☐	☐
Island	☐	☐	☐

	Good	Average	Poor
Basement	☐	☐	☐
Garage	☐	☐	☐

COMMUNITY

	Good	Average	Poor
Immediate Neighborhood	☐	☐	☐
Close to Employment	☐	☐	☐
Close to Shopping	☐	☐	☐
Close to Transportation	☐	☐	☐
Close to Schools / Daycare	☐	☐	☐
Close to Places of Worship	☐	☐	☐
Near Recreational Facilities	☐	☐	☐
Close to Airport	☐	☐	☐
Near Police and Fire Department	☐	☐	☐

Address _____ Price _____

Bedrooms _____ Bathrooms _____ Sq.Ft. _____

Lot Size: _____ Year Built _____ School District _____

Annual Tax _____

EXTERIOR

	Good	Average	Poor
View/Yard/Landscaping	☐	☐	☐
Trees	☐	☐	☐
Lawn (Front)	☐	☐	☐
Lawn (Back)	☐	☐	☐
Fences (condition)	☐	☐	☐
Landscaping (condition)	☐	☐	☐
Irrigation / Sprinkler	☐	☐	☐
	☐	☐	☐
House Type	☐	☐	☐
Exterior Siding	☐	☐	☐
Deck / Patio / Porch	☐	☐	☐
Garage	☐	☐	☐
Window / Doors	☐	☐	☐
Roof / Gutters	☐	☐	☐
Fencing	☐	☐	☐

HOME SYSTEMS

	Good	Average	Poor
Electrical	☐	☐	☐
Air Conditioning / Fans	☐	☐	☐
Heating	☐	☐	☐
Security	☐	☐	☐
Plumbing	☐	☐	☐
Intercom	☐	☐	☐

FEATURES

	Good	Average	Poor
Home Warranty	☐	☐	☐
Energy Saving Features	☐	☐	☐

INTERIOR

	Good	Average	Poor
Walls / Trim / Ceilings	☐	☐	☐
Flooring	☐	☐	☐
Stairs	☐	☐	☐
Storage	☐	☐	☐
Living Room	☐	☐	☐
Family Room	☐	☐	☐
Dining Room	☐	☐	☐

	Good	Average	Poor
Master Bedroom	☐	☐	☐
Bedroom 2	☐	☐	☐
Bedroom 3	☐	☐	☐
Bedroom 4	☐	☐	☐
Master Bathroom	☐	☐	☐
Bathroom 2	☐	☐	☐
Bathroom 3	☐	☐	☐
Bonus / Game Room	☐	☐	☐

	Good	Average	Poor
Kitchen	☐	☐	☐
Cabinets	☐	☐	☐
Countertop	☐	☐	☐
Counter Space	☐	☐	☐
Flooring	☐	☐	☐
Oven / Stove	☐	☐	☐
Microwave	☐	☐	☐
Layout	☐	☐	☐
Light Fixtures	☐	☐	☐
Backsplash	☐	☐	☐
Pantry	☐	☐	☐
Appliances	☐	☐	☐
Island	☐	☐	☐

	Good	Average	Poor
Basement	☐	☐	☐
Garage	☐	☐	☐

COMMUNITY

	Good	Average	Poor
Immediate Neighborhood	☐	☐	☐
Close to Employment	☐	☐	☐
Close to Shopping	☐	☐	☐
Close to Transportation	☐	☐	☐
Close to Schools / Daycare	☐	☐	☐
Close to Places of Worship	☐	☐	☐
Near Recreational Facilities	☐	☐	☐
Close to Airport	☐	☐	☐
Near Police and Fire Department	☐	☐	☐

Address _____ Price _____

Bedrooms _____ Bathrooms _____ Sq.Ft. _____

Lot Size: _____ Year Built _____ School District _____

Annual Tax _____

EXTERIOR

	Good	Average	Poor
View/Yard/Landscaping	☐	☐	☐
Trees	☐	☐	☐
Lawn (Front)	☐	☐	☐
Lawn (Back)	☐	☐	☐
Fences (condition)	☐	☐	☐
Landscaping (condition)	☐	☐	☐
Irrigation / Sprinkler	☐	☐	☐
	☐	☐	☐
House Type	☐	☐	☐
Exterior Siding	☐	☐	☐
Deck / Patio / Porch	☐	☐	☐
Garage	☐	☐	☐
Window / Doors	☐	☐	☐
Roof / Gutters	☐	☐	☐
Fencing	☐	☐	☐

HOME SYSTEMS

	Good	Average	Poor
Electrical	☐	☐	☐
Air Conditioning / Fans	☐	☐	☐
Heating	☐	☐	☐
Security	☐	☐	☐
Plumbing	☐	☐	☐
Intercom	☐	☐	☐

FEATURES

	Good	Average	Poor
Home Warranty	☐	☐	☐
Energy Saving Features	☐	☐	☐

INTERIOR

	Good	Average	Poor
Walls / Trim / Ceilings	☐	☐	☐
Flooring	☐	☐	☐
Stairs	☐	☐	☐
Storage	☐	☐	☐
Living Room	☐	☐	☐
Family Room	☐	☐	☐
Dining Room	☐	☐	☐

	Good	Average	Poor
Master Bedroom	☐	☐	☐
Bedroom 2	☐	☐	☐
Bedroom 3	☐	☐	☐
Bedroom 4	☐	☐	☐
Master Bathroom	☐	☐	☐
Bathroom 2	☐	☐	☐
Bathroom 3	☐	☐	☐
Bonus / Game Room	☐	☐	☐

	Good	Average	Poor
Kitchen			
Cabinets	☐	☐	☐
Countertop	☐	☐	☐
Counter Space	☐	☐	☐
Flooring	☐	☐	☐
Oven / Stove	☐	☐	☐
Microwave	☐	☐	☐
Layout	☐	☐	☐
Light Fixtures	☐	☐	☐
Backsplash	☐	☐	☐
Pantry	☐	☐	☐
Appliances	☐	☐	☐
Island	☐	☐	☐

	Good	Average	Poor
Basement	☐	☐	☐
Garage	☐	☐	☐

COMMUNITY

	Good	Average	Poor
Immediate Neighborhood	☐	☐	☐
Close to Employment	☐	☐	☐
Close to Shopping	☐	☐	☐
Close to Transportation	☐	☐	☐
Close to Schools / Daycare	☐	☐	☐
Close to Places of Worship	☐	☐	☐
Near Recreational Facilities	☐	☐	☐
Close to Airport	☐	☐	☐
Near Police and Fire Department	☐	☐	☐

Address _____ Price _____

Bedrooms _____ Bathrooms _____ Sq.Ft. _____

Lot Size: _____ Year Built _____ School District _____

Annual Tax _____

EXTERIOR

	Good	Average	Poor
View/Yard/Landscaping	☐	☐	☐
Trees	☐	☐	☐
Lawn (Front)	☐	☐	☐
Lawn (Back)	☐	☐	☐
Fences (condition)	☐	☐	☐
Landscaping (condition)	☐	☐	☐
Irrigation / Sprinkler	☐	☐	☐
	☐	☐	☐
House Type	☐	☐	☐
Exterior Siding	☐	☐	☐
Deck / Patio / Porch	☐	☐	☐
Garage	☐	☐	☐
Window / Doors	☐	☐	☐
Roof / Gutters	☐	☐	☐
Fencing	☐	☐	☐

HOME SYSTEMS

	Good	Average	Poor
Electrical	☐	☐	☐
Air Conditioning / Fans	☐	☐	☐
Heating	☐	☐	☐
Security	☐	☐	☐
Plumbing	☐	☐	☐
Intercom	☐	☐	☐

FEATURES

	Good	Average	Poor
Home Warranty	☐	☐	☐
Energy Saving Features	☐	☐	☐

INTERIOR

	Good	Average	Poor
Walls / Trim / Ceilings	☐	☐	☐
Flooring	☐	☐	☐
Stairs	☐	☐	☐
Storage	☐	☐	☐
Living Room	☐	☐	☐
Family Room	☐	☐	☐
Dining Room	☐	☐	☐

	Good	Average	Poor
Master Bedroom	☐	☐	☐
Bedroom 2	☐	☐	☐
Bedroom 3	☐	☐	☐
Bedroom 4	☐	☐	☐
Master Bathroom	☐	☐	☐
Bathroom 2	☐	☐	☐
Bathroom 3	☐	☐	☐
Bonus / Game Room	☐	☐	☐

	Good	Average	Poor
Kitchen	☐	☐	☐
Cabinets	☐	☐	☐
Countertop	☐	☐	☐
Counter Space	☐	☐	☐
Flooring	☐	☐	☐
Oven / Stove	☐	☐	☐
Microwave	☐	☐	☐
Layout	☐	☐	☐
Light Fixtures	☐	☐	☐
Backsplash	☐	☐	☐
Pantry	☐	☐	☐
Appliances	☐	☐	☐
Island	☐	☐	☐

	Good	Average	Poor
Basement	☐	☐	☐
Garage	☐	☐	☐

COMMUNITY

	Good	Average	Poor
Immediate Neighborhood	☐	☐	☐
Close to Employment	☐	☐	☐
Close to Shopping	☐	☐	☐
Close to Transportation	☐	☐	☐
Close to Schools / Daycare	☐	☐	☐
Close to Places of Worship	☐	☐	☐
Near Recreational Facilities	☐	☐	☐
Close to Airport	☐	☐	☐
Near Police and Fire Department	☐	☐	☐

Address _____ Price _____

Bedrooms _____ Bathrooms _____ Sq.Ft. _____

Lot Size: _____ Year Built _____ School District _____

Annual Tax _____

EXTERIOR

	Good	Average	Poor
View/Yard/Landscaping	☐	☐	☐
Trees	☐	☐	☐
Lawn (Front)	☐	☐	☐
Lawn (Back)	☐	☐	☐
Fences (condition)	☐	☐	☐
Landscaping (condition)	☐	☐	☐
Irrigation / Sprinkler	☐	☐	☐
	☐	☐	☐
House Type	☐	☐	☐
Exterior Siding	☐	☐	☐
Deck / Patio / Porch	☐	☐	☐
Garage	☐	☐	☐
Window / Doors	☐	☐	☐
Roof / Gutters	☐	☐	☐
Fencing	☐	☐	☐

HOME SYSTEMS

	Good	Average	Poor
Electrical	☐	☐	☐
Air Conditioning / Fans	☐	☐	☐
Heating	☐	☐	☐
Security	☐	☐	☐
Plumbing	☐	☐	☐
Intercom	☐	☐	☐

FEATURES

	Good	Average	Poor
Home Warranty	☐	☐	☐
Energy Saving Features	☐	☐	☐

INTERIOR

	Good	Average	Poor
Walls / Trim / Ceilings	☐	☐	☐
Flooring	☐	☐	☐
Stairs	☐	☐	☐
Storage	☐	☐	☐
Living Room	☐	☐	☐
Family Room	☐	☐	☐
Dining Room	☐	☐	☐

	Good	Average	Poor
Master Bedroom	☐	☐	☐
Bedroom 2	☐	☐	☐
Bedroom 3	☐	☐	☐
Bedroom 4	☐	☐	☐
Master Bathroom	☐	☐	☐
Bathroom 2	☐	☐	☐
Bathroom 3	☐	☐	☐
Bonus / Game Room	☐	☐	☐

	Good	Average	Poor
Kitchen			
Cabinets	☐	☐	☐
Countertop	☐	☐	☐
Counter Space	☐	☐	☐
Flooring	☐	☐	☐
Oven / Stove	☐	☐	☐
Microwave	☐	☐	☐
Layout	☐	☐	☐
Light Fixtures	☐	☐	☐
Backsplash	☐	☐	☐
Pantry	☐	☐	☐
Appliances	☐	☐	☐
Island	☐	☐	☐

	Good	Average	Poor
Basement	☐	☐	☐
Garage	☐	☐	☐

COMMUNITY

	Good	Average	Poor
Immediate Neighborhood	☐	☐	☐
Close to Employment	☐	☐	☐
Close to Shopping	☐	☐	☐
Close to Transportation	☐	☐	☐
Close to Schools / Daycare	☐	☐	☐
Close to Places of Worship	☐	☐	☐
Near Recreational Facilities	☐	☐	☐
Close to Airport	☐	☐	☐
Near Police and Fire Department	☐	☐	☐

Address _____   Price _____

Bedrooms _____   Bathrooms _____   Sq.Ft. _____

Lot Size: _____   Year Built _____   School District _____

Annual Tax _____

EXTERIOR

	Good	Average	Poor
View/Yard/Landscaping	☐	☐	☐
Trees	☐	☐	☐
Lawn (Front)	☐	☐	☐
Lawn (Back)	☐	☐	☐
Fences (condition)	☐	☐	☐
Landscaping (condition)	☐	☐	☐
Irrigation / Sprinkler	☐	☐	☐
	☐	☐	☐
House Type	☐	☐	☐
Exterior Siding	☐	☐	☐
Deck / Patio / Porch	☐	☐	☐
Garage	☐	☐	☐
Window / Doors	☐	☐	☐
Roof / Gutters	☐	☐	☐
Fencing	☐	☐	☐

HOME SYSTEMS

	Good	Average	Poor
Electrical	☐	☐	☐
Air Conditioning / Fans	☐	☐	☐
Heating	☐	☐	☐
Security	☐	☐	☐
Plumbing	☐	☐	☐
Intercom	☐	☐	☐

FEATURES

	Good	Average	Poor
Home Warranty	☐	☐	☐
Energy Saving Features	☐	☐	☐

INTERIOR

	Good	Average	Poor
Walls / Trim / Ceilings	☐	☐	☐
Flooring	☐	☐	☐
Stairs	☐	☐	☐
Storage	☐	☐	☐
Living Room	☐	☐	☐
Family Room	☐	☐	☐
Dining Room	☐	☐	☐

	Good	Average	Poor
Master Bedroom	☐	☐	☐
Bedroom 2	☐	☐	☐
Bedroom 3	☐	☐	☐
Bedroom 4	☐	☐	☐
Master Bathroom	☐	☐	☐
Bathroom 2	☐	☐	☐
Bathroom 3	☐	☐	☐
Bonus / Game Room	☐	☐	☐

	Good	Average	Poor
Kitchen	☐	☐	☐
Cabinets	☐	☐	☐
Countertop	☐	☐	☐
Counter Space	☐	☐	☐
Flooring	☐	☐	☐
Oven / Stove	☐	☐	☐
Microwave	☐	☐	☐
Layout	☐	☐	☐
Light Fixtures	☐	☐	☐
Backsplash	☐	☐	☐
Pantry	☐	☐	☐
Appliances	☐	☐	☐
Island	☐	☐	☐

	Good	Average	Poor
Basement	☐	☐	☐
Garage	☐	☐	☐

COMMUNITY

	Good	Average	Poor
Immediate Neighborhood	☐	☐	☐
Close to Employment	☐	☐	☐
Close to Shopping	☐	☐	☐
Close to Transportation	☐	☐	☐
Close to Schools / Daycare	☐	☐	☐
Close to Places of Worship	☐	☐	☐
Near Recreational Facilities	☐	☐	☐
Close to Airport	☐	☐	☐
Near Police and Fire Department	☐	☐	☐

Address _____ Price _____

Bedrooms _____ Bathrooms _____ Sq.Ft. _____

Lot Size: _____ Year Built _____ School District _____

Annual Tax _____

EXTERIOR

	Good	Average	Poor
View/Yard/Landscaping	☐	☐	☐
Trees	☐	☐	☐
Lawn (Front)	☐	☐	☐
Lawn (Back)	☐	☐	☐
Fences (condition)	☐	☐	☐
Landscaping (condition)	☐	☐	☐
Irrigation / Sprinkler	☐	☐	☐
House Type	☐	☐	☐
Exterior Siding	☐	☐	☐
Deck / Patio / Porch	☐	☐	☐
Garage	☐	☐	☐
Window / Doors	☐	☐	☐
Roof / Gutters	☐	☐	☐
Fencing	☐	☐	☐

HOME SYSTEMS

	Good	Average	Poor
Electrical	☐	☐	☐
Air Conditioning / Fans	☐	☐	☐
Heating	☐	☐	☐
Security	☐	☐	☐
Plumbing	☐	☐	☐
Intercom	☐	☐	☐

FEATURES

	Good	Average	Poor
Home Warranty	☐	☐	☐
Energy Saving Features	☐	☐	☐

INTERIOR

	Good	Average	Poor
Walls / Trim / Ceilings	☐	☐	☐
Flooring	☐	☐	☐
Stairs	☐	☐	☐
Storage	☐	☐	☐
Living Room	☐	☐	☐
Family Room	☐	☐	☐
Dining Room	☐	☐	☐

	Good	Average	Poor
Master Bedroom	☐	☐	☐
Bedroom 2	☐	☐	☐
Bedroom 3	☐	☐	☐
Bedroom 4	☐	☐	☐
Master Bathroom	☐	☐	☐
Bathroom 2	☐	☐	☐
Bathroom 3	☐	☐	☐
Bonus / Game Room	☐	☐	☐

	Good	Average	Poor
Kitchen	☐	☐	
Cabinets	☐	☐	☐
Countertop	☐	☐	☐
Counter Space	☐	☐	☐
Flooring	☐	☐	☐
Oven / Stove	☐	☐	☐
Microwave	☐	☐	☐
Layout	☐	☐	☐
Light Fixtures	☐	☐	☐
Backsplash	☐	☐	☐
Pantry	☐	☐	☐
Appliances	☐	☐	☐
Island	☐	☐	☐

	Good	Average	Poor
Basement	☐	☐	☐
Garage	☐	☐	☐

COMMUNITY

	Good	Average	Poor
Immediate Neighborhood	☐	☐	☐
Close to Employment	☐	☐	☐
Close to Shopping	☐	☐	☐
Close to Transportation	☐	☐	☐
Close to Schools / Daycare	☐	☐	☐
Close to Places of Worship	☐	☐	☐
Near Recreational Facilities	☐	☐	☐
Close to Airport	☐	☐	☐
Near Police and Fire Department	☐	☐	☐

Address _____ Price _____

Bedrooms _____ Bathrooms _____ Sq.Ft. _____

Lot Size: _____ Year Built _____ School District _____

Annual Tax _____

EXTERIOR

	Good	Average	Poor
View/Yard/Landscaping	☐	☐	☐
Trees	☐	☐	☐
Lawn (Front)	☐	☐	☐
Lawn (Back)	☐	☐	☐
Fences (condition)	☐	☐	☐
Landscaping (condition)	☐	☐	☐
Irrigation / Sprinkler	☐	☐	☐
House Type	☐	☐	☐
Exterior Siding	☐	☐	☐
Deck / Patio / Porch	☐	☐	☐
Garage	☐	☐	☐
Window / Doors	☐	☐	☐
Roof / Gutters	☐	☐	☐
Fencing	☐	☐	☐

HOME SYSTEMS

	Good	Average	Poor
Electrical	☐	☐	☐
Air Conditioning / Fans	☐	☐	☐
Heating	☐	☐	☐
Security	☐	☐	☐
Plumbing	☐	☐	☐
Intercom	☐	☐	☐

FEATURES

	Good	Average	Poor
Home Warranty	☐	☐	☐
Energy Saving Features	☐	☐	☐

INTERIOR

	Good	Average	Poor
Walls / Trim / Ceilings	☐	☐	☐
Flooring	☐	☐	☐
Stairs	☐	☐	☐
Storage	☐	☐	☐
Living Room	☐	☐	☐
Family Room	☐	☐	☐
Dining Room	☐	☐	☐

	Good	Average	Poor
Master Bedroom	☐	☐	☐
Bedroom 2	☐	☐	☐
Bedroom 3	☐	☐	☐
Bedroom 4	☐	☐	☐
Master Bathroom	☐	☐	☐
Bathroom 2	☐	☐	☐
Bathroom 3	☐	☐	☐
Bonus / Game Room	☐	☐	☐

	Good	Average	Poor
Kitchen	☐	☐	☐
Cabinets	☐	☐	☐
Countertop	☐	☐	☐
Counter Space	☐	☐	☐
Flooring	☐	☐	☐
Oven / Stove	☐	☐	☐
Microwave	☐	☐	☐
Layout	☐	☐	☐
Light Fixtures	☐	☐	☐
Backsplash	☐	☐	☐
Pantry	☐	☐	☐
Appliances	☐	☐	☐
Island	☐	☐	☐

	Good	Average	Poor
Basement	☐	☐	☐
Garage	☐	☐	☐

COMMUNITY

	Good	Average	Poor
Immediate Neighborhood	☐	☐	☐
Close to Employment	☐	☐	☐
Close to Shopping	☐	☐	☐
Close to Transportation	☐	☐	☐
Close to Schools / Daycare	☐	☐	☐
Close to Places of Worship	☐	☐	☐
Near Recreational Facilities	☐	☐	☐
Close to Airport	☐	☐	☐
Near Police and Fire Department	☐	☐	☐

Address _____ Price _____

Bedrooms _____ Bathrooms _____ Sq.Ft. _____

Lot Size: _____ Year Built _____ School District _____

Annual Tax _____

EXTERIOR

	Good	Average	Poor
View/Yard/Landscaping	☐	☐	☐
Trees	☐	☐	☐
Lawn (Front)	☐	☐	☐
Lawn (Back)	☐	☐	☐
Fences (condition)	☐	☐	☐
Landscaping (condition)	☐	☐	☐
Irrigation / Sprinkler	☐	☐	☐
House Type	☐	☐	☐
Exterior Siding	☐	☐	☐
Deck / Patio / Porch	☐	☐	☐
Garage	☐	☐	☐
Window / Doors	☐	☐	☐
Roof / Gutters	☐	☐	☐
Fencing	☐	☐	☐

HOME SYSTEMS

	Good	Average	Poor
Electrical	☐	☐	☐
Air Conditioning / Fans	☐	☐	☐
Heating	☐	☐	☐
Security	☐	☐	☐
Plumbing	☐	☐	☐
Intercom	☐	☐	☐

FEATURES

	Good	Average	Poor
Home Warranty	☐	☐	☐
Energy Saving Features	☐	☐	☐

INTERIOR

	Good	Average	Poor
Walls / Trim / Ceilings	☐	☐	☐
Flooring	☐	☐	☐
Stairs	☐	☐	☐
Storage	☐	☐	☐
Living Room	☐	☐	☐
Family Room	☐	☐	☐
Dining Room	☐	☐	☐

	Good	Average	Poor
Master Bedroom	☐	☐	☐
Bedroom 2	☐	☐	☐
Bedroom 3	☐	☐	☐
Bedroom 4	☐	☐	☐
Master Bathroom	☐	☐	☐
Bathroom 2	☐	☐	☐
Bathroom 3	☐	☐	☐
Bonus / Game Room	☐	☐	☐

	Good	Average	Poor
Kitchen			
Cabinets	☐	☐	☐
Countertop	☐	☐	☐
Counter Space	☐	☐	☐
Flooring	☐	☐	☐
Oven / Stove	☐	☐	☐
Microwave	☐	☐	☐
Layout	☐	☐	☐
Light Fixtures	☐	☐	☐
Backsplash	☐	☐	☐
Pantry	☐	☐	☐
Appliances	☐	☐	☐
Island	☐	☐	☐

	Good	Average	Poor
Basement	☐	☐	☐
Garage	☐	☐	☐

COMMUNITY

	Good	Average	Poor
Immediate Neighborhood	☐	☐	☐
Close to Employment	☐	☐	☐
Close to Shopping	☐	☐	☐
Close to Transportation	☐	☐	☐
Close to Schools / Daycare	☐	☐	☐
Close to Places of Worship	☐	☐	☐
Near Recreational Facilities	☐	☐	☐
Close to Airport	☐	☐	☐
Near Police and Fire Department	☐	☐	☐

Address _____ Price _____

Bedrooms _____ Bathrooms _____ Sq.Ft. _____

Lot Size: _____ Year Built _____ School District _____

Annual Tax _____

EXTERIOR

	Good	Average	Poor
View/Yard/Landscaping	☐	☐	☐
Trees	☐	☐	☐
Lawn (Front)	☐	☐	☐
Lawn (Back)	☐	☐	☐
Fences (condition)	☐	☐	☐
Landscaping (condition)	☐	☐	☐
Irrigation / Sprinkler	☐	☐	☐
	☐	☐	☐
House Type	☐	☐	☐
Exterior Siding	☐	☐	☐
Deck / Patio / Porch	☐	☐	☐
Garage	☐	☐	☐
Window / Doors	☐	☐	☐
Roof / Gutters	☐	☐	☐
Fencing	☐	☐	☐

HOME SYSTEMS

	Good	Average	Poor
Electrical	☐	☐	☐
Air Conditioning / Fans	☐	☐	☐
Heating	☐	☐	☐
Security	☐	☐	☐
Plumbing	☐	☐	☐
Intercom	☐	☐	☐

FEATURES

	Good	Average	Poor
Home Warranty	☐	☐	☐
Energy Saving Features	☐	☐	☐

INTERIOR

	Good	Average	Poor
Walls / Trim / Ceilings	☐	☐	☐
Flooring	☐	☐	☐
Stairs	☐	☐	☐
Storage	☐	☐	☐
Living Room	☐	☐	☐
Family Room	☐	☐	☐
Dining Room	☐	☐	☐

	Good	Average	Poor
Master Bedroom	☐	☐	☐
Bedroom 2	☐	☐	☐
Bedroom 3	☐	☐	☐
Bedroom 4	☐	☐	☐
Master Bathroom	☐	☐	☐
Bathroom 2	☐	☐	☐
Bathroom 3	☐	☐	☐
Bonus / Game Room	☐	☐	☐

	Good	Average	Poor
Kitchen	☐	☐	☐
Cabinets	☐	☐	☐
Countertop	☐	☐	☐
Counter Space	☐	☐	☐
Flooring	☐	☐	☐
Oven / Stove	☐	☐	☐
Microwave	☐	☐	☐
Layout	☐	☐	☐
Light Fixtures	☐	☐	☐
Backsplash	☐	☐	☐
Pantry	☐	☐	☐
Appliances	☐	☐	☐
Island	☐	☐	☐

	Good	Average	Poor
Basement	☐	☐	☐
Garage	☐	☐	☐

COMMUNITY

	Good	Average	Poor
Immediate Neighborhood	☐	☐	☐
Close to Employment	☐	☐	☐
Close to Shopping	☐	☐	☐
Close to Transportation	☐	☐	☐
Close to Schools / Daycare	☐	☐	☐
Close to Places of Worship	☐	☐	☐
Near Recreational Facilities	☐	☐	☐
Close to Airport	☐	☐	☐
Near Police and Fire Department	☐	☐	☐

Address _____   Price _____

Bedrooms _____   Bathrooms _____   Sq.Ft. _____

Lot Size: _____   Year Built _____   School District _____

Annual Tax _____

EXTERIOR

	Good	Average	Poor
View/Yard/Landscaping	☐	☐	☐
Trees	☐	☐	☐
Lawn (Front)	☐	☐	☐
Lawn (Back)	☐	☐	☐
Fences (condition)	☐	☐	☐
Landscaping (condition)	☐	☐	☐
Irrigation / Sprinkler	☐	☐	☐
	☐	☐	☐
House Type	☐	☐	☐
Exterior Siding	☐	☐	☐
Deck / Patio / Porch	☐	☐	☐
Garage	☐	☐	☐
Window / Doors	☐	☐	☐
Roof / Gutters	☐	☐	☐
Fencing	☐	☐	☐

HOME SYSTEMS

	Good	Average	Poor
Electrical	☐	☐	☐
Air Conditioning / Fans	☐	☐	☐
Heating	☐	☐	☐
Security	☐	☐	☐
Plumbing	☐	☐	☐
Intercom	☐	☐	☐

FEATURES

	Good	Average	Poor
Home Warranty	☐	☐	☐
Energy Saving Features	☐	☐	☐

INTERIOR

	Good	Average	Poor
Walls / Trim / Ceilings	☐	☐	☐
Flooring	☐	☐	☐
Stairs	☐	☐	☐
Storage	☐	☐	☐
Living Room	☐	☐	☐
Family Room	☐	☐	☐
Dining Room	☐	☐	☐

	Good	Average	Poor
Master Bedroom	☐	☐	☐
Bedroom 2	☐	☐	☐
Bedroom 3	☐	☐	☐
Bedroom 4	☐	☐	☐
Master Bathroom	☐	☐	☐
Bathroom 2	☐	☐	☐
Bathroom 3	☐	☐	☐
Bonus / Game Room	☐	☐	☐

	Good	Average	Poor
Kitchen	☐	☐	☐
Cabinets	☐	☐	☐
Countertop	☐	☐	☐
Counter Space	☐	☐	☐
Flooring	☐	☐	☐
Oven / Stove	☐	☐	☐
Microwave	☐	☐	☐
Layout	☐	☐	☐
Light Fixtures	☐	☐	☐
Backsplash	☐	☐	☐
Pantry	☐	☐	☐
Appliances	☐	☐	☐
Island	☐	☐	☐

	Good	Average	Poor
Basement	☐	☐	☐
Garage	☐	☐	☐

COMMUNITY

	Good	Average	Poor
Immediate Neighborhood	☐	☐	☐
Close to Employment	☐	☐	☐
Close to Shopping	☐	☐	☐
Close to Transportation	☐	☐	☐
Close to Schools / Daycare	☐	☐	☐
Close to Places of Worship	☐	☐	☐
Near Recreational Facilities	☐	☐	☐
Close to Airport	☐	☐	☐
Near Police and Fire Department	☐	☐	☐

Address _____ Price _____

Bedrooms _____ Bathrooms _____ Sq.Ft. _____

Lot Size: _____ Year Built _____ School District _____

Annual Tax _____

EXTERIOR

	Good	Average	Poor
View/Yard/Landscaping	☐	☐	☐
Trees	☐	☐	☐
Lawn (Front)	☐	☐	☐
Lawn (Back)	☐	☐	☐
Fences (condition)	☐	☐	☐
Landscaping (condition)	☐	☐	☐
Irrigation / Sprinkler	☐	☐	☐
	☐	☐	☐
House Type	☐	☐	☐
Exterior Siding	☐	☐	☐
Deck / Patio / Porch	☐	☐	☐
Garage	☐	☐	☐
Window / Doors	☐	☐	☐
Roof / Gutters	☐	☐	☐
Fencing	☐	☐	☐

HOME SYSTEMS

	Good	Average	Poor
Electrical	☐	☐	☐
Air Conditioning / Fans	☐	☐	☐
Heating	☐	☐	☐
Security	☐	☐	☐
Plumbing	☐	☐	☐
Intercom	☐	☐	☐

FEATURES

	Good	Average	Poor
Home Warranty	☐	☐	☐
Energy Saving Features	☐	☐	☐

INTERIOR

	Good	Average	Poor
Walls / Trim / Ceilings	☐	☐	☐
Flooring	☐	☐	☐
Stairs	☐	☐	☐
Storage	☐	☐	☐
Living Room	☐	☐	☐
Family Room	☐	☐	☐
Dining Room	☐	☐	☐

	Good	Average	Poor
Master Bedroom	☐	☐	☐
Bedroom 2	☐	☐	☐
Bedroom 3	☐	☐	☐
Bedroom 4	☐	☐	☐
Master Bathroom	☐	☐	☐
Bathroom 2	☐	☐	☐
Bathroom 3	☐	☐	☐
Bonus / Game Room	☐	☐	☐

	Good	Average	Poor
Kitchen			
Cabinets	☐	☐	☐
Countertop	☐	☐	☐
Counter Space	☐	☐	☐
Flooring	☐	☐	☐
Oven / Stove	☐	☐	☐
Microwave	☐	☐	☐
Layout	☐	☐	☐
Light Fixtures	☐	☐	☐
Backsplash	☐	☐	☐
Pantry	☐	☐	☐
Appliances	☐	☐	☐
Island	☐	☐	☐

	Good	Average	Poor
Basement	☐	☐	☐
Garage	☐	☐	☐

COMMUNITY

	Good	Average	Poor
Immediate Neighborhood	☐	☐	☐
Close to Employment	☐	☐	☐
Close to Shopping	☐	☐	☐
Close to Transportation	☐	☐	☐
Close to Schools / Daycare	☐	☐	☐
Close to Places of Worship	☐	☐	☐
Near Recreational Facilities	☐	☐	☐
Close to Airport	☐	☐	☐
Near Police and Fire Department	☐	☐	☐

Address _____ Price _____

Bedrooms _____ Bathrooms _____ Sq.Ft. _____

Lot Size: _____ Year Built _____ School District _____

Annual Tax _____

EXTERIOR

	Good	Average	Poor
View/Yard/Landscaping	☐	☐	☐
Trees	☐	☐	☐
Lawn (Front)	☐	☐	☐
Lawn (Back)	☐	☐	☐
Fences (condition)	☐	☐	☐
Landscaping (condition)	☐	☐	☐
Irrigation / Sprinkler	☐	☐	☐
House Type	☐	☐	☐
Exterior Siding	☐	☐	☐
Deck / Patio / Porch	☐	☐	☐
Garage	☐	☐	☐
Window / Doors	☐	☐	☐
Roof / Gutters	☐	☐	☐
Fencing	☐	☐	☐

HOME SYSTEMS

	Good	Average	Poor
Electrical	☐	☐	☐
Air Conditioning / Fans	☐	☐	☐
Heating	☐	☐	☐
Security	☐	☐	☐
Plumbing	☐	☐	☐
Intercom	☐	☐	☐

FEATURES

	Good	Average	Poor
Home Warranty	☐	☐	☐
Energy Saving Features	☐	☐	☐

INTERIOR

	Good	Average	Poor
Walls / Trim / Ceilings	☐	☐	☐
Flooring	☐	☐	☐
Stairs	☐	☐	☐
Storage	☐	☐	☐
Living Room	☐	☐	☐
Family Room	☐	☐	☐
Dining Room	☐	☐	☐

	Good	Average	Poor
Master Bedroom	☐	☐	☐
Bedroom 2	☐	☐	☐
Bedroom 3	☐	☐	☐
Bedroom 4	☐	☐	☐
Master Bathroom	☐	☐	☐
Bathroom 2	☐	☐	☐
Bathroom 3	☐	☐	☐
Bonus / Game Room	☐	☐	☐

	Good	Average	Poor
Kitchen			
Cabinets	☐	☐	☐
Countertop	☐	☐	☐
Counter Space	☐	☐	☐
Flooring	☐	☐	☐
Oven / Stove	☐	☐	☐
Microwave	☐	☐	☐
Layout	☐	☐	☐
Light Fixtures	☐	☐	☐
Backsplash	☐	☐	☐
Pantry	☐	☐	☐
Appliances	☐	☐	☐
Island	☐	☐	☐

	Good	Average	Poor
Basement	☐	☐	☐
Garage	☐	☐	☐

COMMUNITY

	Good	Average	Poor
Immediate Neighborhood	☐	☐	☐
Close to Employment	☐	☐	☐
Close to Shopping	☐	☐	☐
Close to Transportation	☐	☐	☐
Close to Schools / Daycare	☐	☐	☐
Close to Places of Worship	☐	☐	☐
Near Recreational Facilities	☐	☐	☐
Close to Airport	☐	☐	☐
Near Police and Fire Department	☐	☐	☐

Address _____ Price _____

Bedrooms _____ Bathrooms _____ Sq.Ft. _____

Lot Size: _____ Year Built _____ School District _____

Annual Tax _____

EXTERIOR

	Good	Average	Poor
View/Yard/Landscaping	☐	☐	☐
Trees	☐	☐	☐
Lawn (Front)	☐	☐	☐
Lawn (Back)	☐	☐	☐
Fences (condition)	☐	☐	☐
Landscaping (condition)	☐	☐	☐
Irrigation / Sprinkler	☐	☐	☐
House Type	☐	☐	☐
Exterior Siding	☐	☐	☐
Deck / Patio / Porch	☐	☐	☐
Garage	☐	☐	☐
Window / Doors	☐	☐	☐
Roof / Gutters	☐	☐	☐
Fencing	☐	☐	☐

HOME SYSTEMS

	Good	Average	Poor
Electrical	☐	☐	☐
Air Conditioning / Fans	☐	☐	☐
Heating	☐	☐	☐
Security	☐	☐	☐
Plumbing	☐	☐	☐
Intercom	☐	☐	☐

FEATURES

	Good	Average	Poor
Home Warranty	☐	☐	☐
Energy Saving Features	☐	☐	☐

INTERIOR

	Good	Average	Poor
Walls / Trim / Ceilings	☐	☐	☐
Flooring	☐	☐	☐
Stairs	☐	☐	☐
Storage	☐	☐	☐
Living Room	☐	☐	☐
Family Room	☐	☐	☐
Dining Room	☐	☐	☐

	Good	Average	Poor
Master Bedroom	☐	☐	☐
Bedroom 2	☐	☐	☐
Bedroom 3	☐	☐	☐
Bedroom 4	☐	☐	☐
Master Bathroom	☐	☐	☐
Bathroom 2	☐	☐	☐
Bathroom 3	☐	☐	☐
Bonus / Game Room	☐	☐	☐

	Good	Average	Poor
Kitchen	☐	☐	☐
Cabinets	☐	☐	☐
Countertop	☐	☐	☐
Counter Space	☐	☐	☐
Flooring	☐	☐	☐
Oven / Stove	☐	☐	☐
Microwave	☐	☐	☐
Layout	☐	☐	☐
Light Fixtures	☐	☐	☐
Backsplash	☐	☐	☐
Pantry	☐	☐	☐
Appliances	☐	☐	☐
Island	☐	☐	☐

	Good	Average	Poor
Basement	☐	☐	☐
Garage	☐	☐	☐

COMMUNITY

	Good	Average	Poor
Immediate Neighborhood	☐	☐	☐
Close to Employment	☐	☐	☐
Close to Shopping	☐	☐	☐
Close to Transportation	☐	☐	☐
Close to Schools / Daycare	☐	☐	☐
Close to Places of Worship	☐	☐	☐
Near Recreational Facilities	☐	☐	☐
Close to Airport	☐	☐	☐
Near Police and Fire Department	☐	☐	☐

Address _____   Price _____

Bedrooms _____   Bathrooms _____   Sq.Ft. _____

Lot Size: _____   Year Built _____   School District _____

Annual Tax _____

EXTERIOR

	Good	Average	Poor
View/Yard/Landscaping	☐	☐	☐
Trees	☐	☐	☐
Lawn (Front)	☐	☐	☐
Lawn (Back)	☐	☐	☐
Fences (condition)	☐	☐	☐
Landscaping (condition)	☐	☐	☐
Irrigation / Sprinkler	☐	☐	☐
House Type	☐	☐	☐
Exterior Siding	☐	☐	☐
Deck / Patio / Porch	☐	☐	☐
Garage	☐	☐	☐
Window / Doors	☐	☐	☐
Roof / Gutters	☐	☐	☐
Fencing	☐	☐	☐

HOME SYSTEMS

	Good	Average	Poor
Electrical	☐	☐	☐
Air Conditioning / Fans	☐	☐	☐
Heating	☐	☐	☐
Security	☐	☐	☐
Plumbing	☐	☐	☐
Intercom	☐	☐	☐

FEATURES

	Good	Average	Poor
Home Warranty	☐	☐	☐
Energy Saving Features	☐	☐	☐

INTERIOR

	Good	Average	Poor
Walls / Trim / Ceilings	☐	☐	☐
Flooring	☐	☐	☐
Stairs	☐	☐	☐
Storage	☐	☐	☐
Living Room	☐	☐	☐
Family Room	☐	☐	☐
Dining Room	☐	☐	☐

	Good	Average	Poor
Master Bedroom	☐	☐	☐
Bedroom 2	☐	☐	☐
Bedroom 3	☐	☐	☐
Bedroom 4	☐	☐	☐
Master Bathroom	☐	☐	☐
Bathroom 2	☐	☐	☐
Bathroom 3	☐	☐	☐
Bonus / Game Room	☐	☐	☐

	Good	Average	Poor
Kitchen	☐	☐	☐
Cabinets	☐	☐	☐
Countertop	☐	☐	☐
Counter Space	☐	☐	☐
Flooring	☐	☐	☐
Oven / Stove	☐	☐	☐
Microwave	☐	☐	☐
Layout	☐	☐	☐
Light Fixtures	☐	☐	☐
Backsplash	☐	☐	☐
Pantry	☐	☐	☐
Appliances	☐	☐	☐
Island	☐	☐	☐

	Good	Average	Poor
Basement	☐	☐	☐
Garage	☐	☐	☐

COMMUNITY

	Good	Average	Poor
Immediate Neighborhood	☐	☐	☐
Close to Employment	☐	☐	☐
Close to Shopping	☐	☐	☐
Close to Transportation	☐	☐	☐
Close to Schools / Daycare	☐	☐	☐
Close to Places of Worship	☐	☐	☐
Near Recreational Facilities	☐	☐	☐
Close to Airport	☐	☐	☐
Near Police and Fire Department	☐	☐	☐

Address _____ Price _____

Bedrooms _____ Bathrooms _____ Sq.Ft. _____

Lot Size: _____ Year Built _____ School District _____

Annual Tax _____

EXTERIOR

	Good	Average	Poor
View/Yard/Landscaping	☐	☐	☐
Trees	☐	☐	☐
Lawn (Front)	☐	☐	☐
Lawn (Back)	☐	☐	☐
Fences (condition)	☐	☐	☐
Landscaping (condition)	☐	☐	☐
Irrigation / Sprinkler	☐	☐	☐
	☐	☐	☐
House Type	☐	☐	☐
Exterior Siding	☐	☐	☐
Deck / Patio / Porch	☐	☐	☐
Garage	☐	☐	☐
Window / Doors	☐	☐	☐
Roof / Gutters	☐	☐	☐
Fencing	☐	☐	☐

HOME SYSTEMS

	Good	Average	Poor
Electrical	☐	☐	☐
Air Conditioning / Fans	☐	☐	☐
Heating	☐	☐	☐
Security	☐	☐	☐
Plumbing	☐	☐	☐
Intercom	☐	☐	☐

FEATURES

	Good	Average	Poor
Home Warranty	☐	☐	☐
Energy Saving Features	☐	☐	☐

INTERIOR

	Good	Average	Poor
Walls / Trim / Ceilings	☐	☐	☐
Flooring	☐	☐	☐
Stairs	☐	☐	☐
Storage	☐	☐	☐
Living Room	☐	☐	☐
Family Room	☐	☐	☐
Dining Room	☐	☐	☐

	Good	Average	Poor
Master Bedroom	☐	☐	☐
Bedroom 2	☐	☐	☐
Bedroom 3	☐	☐	☐
Bedroom 4	☐	☐	☐
Master Bathroom	☐	☐	☐
Bathroom 2	☐	☐	☐
Bathroom 3	☐	☐	☐
Bonus / Game Room	☐	☐	☐

	Good	Average	Poor
Kitchen	☐	☐	☐
Cabinets	☐	☐	☐
Countertop	☐	☐	☐
Counter Space	☐	☐	☐
Flooring	☐	☐	☐
Oven / Stove	☐	☐	☐
Microwave	☐	☐	☐
Layout	☐	☐	☐
Light Fixtures	☐	☐	☐
Backsplash	☐	☐	☐
Pantry	☐	☐	☐
Appliances	☐	☐	☐
Island	☐	☐	☐

	Good	Average	Poor
Basement	☐	☐	☐
Garage	☐	☐	☐

COMMUNITY

	Good	Average	Poor
Immediate Neighborhood	☐	☐	☐
Close to Employment	☐	☐	☐
Close to Shopping	☐	☐	☐
Close to Transportation	☐	☐	☐
Close to Schools / Daycare	☐	☐	☐
Close to Places of Worship	☐	☐	☐
Near Recreational Facilities	☐	☐	☐
Close to Airport	☐	☐	☐
Near Police and Fire Department	☐	☐	☐

Address _____ Price _____

Bedrooms _____ Bathrooms _____ Sq.Ft. _____

Lot Size: _____ Year Built _____ School District _____

Annual Tax _____

EXTERIOR

	Good	Average	Poor
View/Yard/Landscaping	☐	☐	☐
Trees	☐	☐	☐
Lawn (Front)	☐	☐	☐
Lawn (Back)	☐	☐	☐
Fences (condition)	☐	☐	☐
Landscaping (condition)	☐	☐	☐
Irrigation / Sprinkler	☐	☐	☐
	☐	☐	☐
House Type	☐	☐	☐
Exterior Siding	☐	☐	☐
Deck / Patio / Porch	☐	☐	☐
Garage	☐	☐	☐
Window / Doors	☐	☐	☐
Roof / Gutters	☐	☐	☐
Fencing	☐	☐	☐

HOME SYSTEMS

	Good	Average	Poor
Electrical	☐	☐	☐
Air Conditioning / Fans	☐	☐	☐
Heating	☐	☐	☐
Security	☐	☐	☐
Plumbing	☐	☐	☐
Intercom	☐	☐	☐

FEATURES

	Good	Average	Poor
Home Warranty	☐	☐	☐
Energy Saving Features	☐	☐	☐

INTERIOR

	Good	Average	Poor
Walls / Trim / Ceilings	☐	☐	☐
Flooring	☐	☐	☐
Stairs	☐	☐	☐
Storage	☐	☐	☐
Living Room	☐	☐	☐
Family Room	☐	☐	☐
Dining Room	☐	☐	☐

	Good	Average	Poor
Master Bedroom	☐	☐	☐
Bedroom 2	☐	☐	☐
Bedroom 3	☐	☐	☐
Bedroom 4	☐	☐	☐
Master Bathroom	☐	☐	☐
Bathroom 2	☐	☐	☐
Bathroom 3	☐	☐	☐
Bonus / Game Room	☐	☐	☐

	Good	Average	Poor
Kitchen			
Cabinets	☐	☐	☐
Countertop	☐	☐	☐
Counter Space	☐	☐	☐
Flooring	☐	☐	☐
Oven / Stove	☐	☐	☐
Microwave	☐	☐	☐
Layout	☐	☐	☐
Light Fixtures	☐	☐	☐
Backsplash	☐	☐	☐
Pantry	☐	☐	☐
Appliances	☐	☐	☐
Island	☐	☐	☐

	Good	Average	Poor
Basement	☐	☐	☐
Garage	☐	☐	☐

COMMUNITY

	Good	Average	Poor
Immediate Neighborhood	☐	☐	☐
Close to Employment	☐	☐	☐
Close to Shopping	☐	☐	☐
Close to Transportation	☐	☐	☐
Close to Schools / Daycare	☐	☐	☐
Close to Places of Worship	☐	☐	☐
Near Recreational Facilities	☐	☐	☐
Close to Airport	☐	☐	☐
Near Police and Fire Department	☐	☐	☐

Address _____ Price _____

Bedrooms _____ Bathrooms _____ Sq.Ft. _____

Lot Size: _____ Year Built _____ School District _____

Annual Tax _____

EXTERIOR

	Good	Average	Poor
View/Yard/Landscaping	☐	☐	☐
Trees	☐	☐	☐
Lawn (Front)	☐	☐	☐
Lawn (Back)	☐	☐	☐
Fences (condition)	☐	☐	☐
Landscaping (condition)	☐	☐	☐
Irrigation / Sprinkler	☐	☐	☐
	☐	☐	☐
House Type	☐	☐	☐
Exterior Siding	☐	☐	☐
Deck / Patio / Porch	☐	☐	☐
Garage	☐	☐	☐
Window / Doors	☐	☐	☐
Roof / Gutters	☐	☐	☐
Fencing	☐	☐	☐

HOME SYSTEMS

	Good	Average	Poor
Electrical	☐	☐	☐
Air Conditioning / Fans	☐	☐	☐
Heating	☐	☐	☐
Security	☐	☐	☐
Plumbing	☐	☐	☐
Intercom	☐	☐	☐

FEATURES

	Good	Average	Poor
Home Warranty	☐	☐	☐
Energy Saving Features	☐	☐	☐

INTERIOR

	Good	Average	Poor
Walls / Trim / Ceilings	☐	☐	☐
Flooring	☐	☐	☐
Stairs	☐	☐	☐
Storage	☐	☐	☐
Living Room	☐	☐	☐
Family Room	☐	☐	☐
Dining Room	☐	☐	☐

	Good	Average	Poor
Master Bedroom	☐	☐	☐
Bedroom 2	☐	☐	☐
Bedroom 3	☐	☐	☐
Bedroom 4	☐	☐	☐
Master Bathroom	☐	☐	☐
Bathroom 2	☐	☐	☐
Bathroom 3	☐	☐	☐
Bonus / Game Room	☐	☐	☐

Kitchen

	Good	Average	Poor
Cabinets	☐	☐	☐
Countertop	☐	☐	☐
Counter Space	☐	☐	☐
Flooring	☐	☐	☐
Oven / Stove	☐	☐	☐
Microwave	☐	☐	☐
Layout	☐	☐	☐
Light Fixtures	☐	☐	☐
Backsplash	☐	☐	☐
Pantry	☐	☐	☐
Appliances	☐	☐	☐
Island	☐	☐	☐

	Good	Average	Poor
Basement	☐	☐	☐
Garage	☐	☐	☐

COMMUNITY

	Good	Average	Poor
Immediate Neighborhood	☐	☐	☐
Close to Employment	☐	☐	☐
Close to Shopping	☐	☐	☐
Close to Transportation	☐	☐	☐
Close to Schools / Daycare	☐	☐	☐
Close to Places of Worship	☐	☐	☐
Near Recreational Facilities	☐	☐	☐
Close to Airport	☐	☐	☐
Near Police and Fire Department	☐	☐	☐

Address _____ Price _____

Bedrooms _____ Bathrooms _____ Sq.Ft. _____

Lot Size: _____ Year Built _____ School District _____

Annual Tax _____

EXTERIOR

	Good	Average	Poor
View/Yard/Landscaping	☐	☐	☐
Trees	☐	☐	☐
Lawn (Front)	☐	☐	☐
Lawn (Back)	☐	☐	☐
Fences (condition)	☐	☐	☐
Landscaping (condition)	☐	☐	☐
Irrigation / Sprinkler	☐	☐	☐
	☐	☐	☐
House Type	☐	☐	☐
Exterior Siding	☐	☐	☐
Deck / Patio / Porch	☐	☐	☐
Garage	☐	☐	☐
Window / Doors	☐	☐	☐
Roof / Gutters	☐	☐	☐
Fencing	☐	☐	☐

HOME SYSTEMS

	Good	Average	Poor
Electrical	☐	☐	☐
Air Conditioning / Fans	☐	☐	☐
Heating	☐	☐	☐
Security	☐	☐	☐
Plumbing	☐	☐	☐
Intercom	☐	☐	☐

FEATURES

	Good	Average	Poor
Home Warranty	☐	☐	☐
Energy Saving Features	☐	☐	☐

INTERIOR

	Good	Average	Poor
Walls / Trim / Ceilings	☐	☐	☐
Flooring	☐	☐	☐
Stairs	☐	☐	☐
Storage	☐	☐	☐
Living Room	☐	☐	☐
Family Room	☐	☐	☐
Dining Room	☐	☐	☐

	Good	Average	Poor
Master Bedroom	☐	☐	☐
Bedroom 2	☐	☐	☐
Bedroom 3	☐	☐	☐
Bedroom 4	☐	☐	☐
Master Bathroom	☐	☐	☐
Bathroom 2	☐	☐	☐
Bathroom 3	☐	☐	☐
Bonus / Game Room	☐	☐	☐

	Good	Average	Poor
Kitchen	☐	☐	☐
Cabinets	☐	☐	☐
Countertop	☐	☐	☐
Counter Space	☐	☐	☐
Flooring	☐	☐	☐
Oven / Stove	☐	☐	☐
Microwave	☐	☐	☐
Layout	☐	☐	☐
Light Fixtures	☐	☐	☐
Backsplash	☐	☐	☐
Pantry	☐	☐	☐
Appliances	☐	☐	☐
Island	☐	☐	☐

	Good	Average	Poor
Basement	☐	☐	☐
Garage	☐	☐	☐

COMMUNITY

	Good	Average	Poor
Immediate Neighborhood	☐	☐	☐
Close to Employment	☐	☐	☐
Close to Shopping	☐	☐	☐
Close to Transportation	☐	☐	☐
Close to Schools / Daycare	☐	☐	☐
Close to Places of Worship	☐	☐	☐
Near Recreational Facilities	☐	☐	☐
Close to Airport	☐	☐	☐
Near Police and Fire Department	☐	☐	☐

Address _____ Price _____

Bedrooms _____ Bathrooms _____ Sq.Ft. _____

Lot Size: _____ Year Built _____ School District _____

Annual Tax _____

EXTERIOR

	Good	Average	Poor
View/Yard/Landscaping	☐	☐	☐
Trees	☐	☐	☐
Lawn (Front)	☐	☐	☐
Lawn (Back)	☐	☐	☐
Fences (condition)	☐	☐	☐
Landscaping (condition)	☐	☐	☐
Irrigation / Sprinkler	☐	☐	☐
	☐	☐	☐
House Type	☐	☐	☐
Exterior Siding	☐	☐	☐
Deck / Patio / Porch	☐	☐	☐
Garage	☐	☐	☐
Window / Doors	☐	☐	☐
Roof / Gutters	☐	☐	☐
Fencing	☐	☐	☐

HOME SYSTEMS

	Good	Average	Poor
Electrical	☐	☐	☐
Air Conditioning / Fans	☐	☐	☐
Heating	☐	☐	☐
Security	☐	☐	☐
Plumbing	☐	☐	☐
Intercom	☐	☐	☐

FEATURES

	Good	Average	Poor
Home Warranty	☐	☐	☐
Energy Saving Features	☐	☐	☐

INTERIOR

	Good	Average	Poor
Walls / Trim / Ceilings	☐	☐	☐
Flooring	☐	☐	☐
Stairs	☐	☐	☐
Storage	☐	☐	☐
Living Room	☐	☐	☐
Family Room	☐	☐	☐
Dining Room	☐	☐	☐

	Good	Average	Poor
Master Bedroom	☐	☐	☐
Bedroom 2	☐	☐	☐
Bedroom 3	☐	☐	☐
Bedroom 4	☐	☐	☐
Master Bathroom	☐	☐	☐
Bathroom 2	☐	☐	☐
Bathroom 3	☐	☐	☐
Bonus / Game Room	☐	☐	☐

	Good	Average	Poor
Kitchen	☐	☐	☐
Cabinets	☐	☐	☐
Countertop	☐	☐	☐
Counter Space	☐	☐	☐
Flooring	☐	☐	☐
Oven / Stove	☐	☐	☐
Microwave	☐	☐	☐
Layout	☐	☐	☐
Light Fixtures	☐	☐	☐
Backsplash	☐	☐	☐
Pantry	☐	☐	☐
Appliances	☐	☐	☐
Island	☐	☐	☐

	Good	Average	Poor
Basement	☐	☐	☐
Garage	☐	☐	☐

COMMUNITY

	Good	Average	Poor
Immediate Neighborhood	☐	☐	☐
Close to Employment	☐	☐	☐
Close to Shopping	☐	☐	☐
Close to Transportation	☐	☐	☐
Close to Schools / Daycare	☐	☐	☐
Close to Places of Worship	☐	☐	☐
Near Recreational Facilities	☐	☐	☐
Close to Airport	☐	☐	☐
Near Police and Fire Department	☐	☐	☐

Address _____ Price _____

Bedrooms _____ Bathrooms _____ Sq.Ft. _____

Lot Size: _____ Year Built _____ School District _____

Annual Tax _____

EXTERIOR

	Good	Average	Poor
View/Yard/Landscaping	☐	☐	☐
Trees	☐	☐	☐
Lawn (Front)	☐	☐	☐
Lawn (Back)	☐	☐	☐
Fences (condition)	☐	☐	☐
Landscaping (condition)	☐	☐	☐
Irrigation / Sprinkler	☐	☐	☐
	☐	☐	☐
House Type	☐	☐	☐
Exterior Siding	☐	☐	☐
Deck / Patio / Porch	☐	☐	☐
Garage	☐	☐	☐
Window / Doors	☐	☐	☐
Roof / Gutters	☐	☐	☐
Fencing	☐	☐	☐

HOME SYSTEMS

	Good	Average	Poor
Electrical	☐	☐	☐
Air Conditioning / Fans	☐	☐	☐
Heating	☐	☐	☐
Security	☐	☐	☐
Plumbing	☐	☐	☐
Intercom	☐	☐	☐

FEATURES

	Good	Average	Poor
Home Warranty	☐	☐	☐
Energy Saving Features	☐	☐	☐

INTERIOR

	Good	Average	Poor
Walls / Trim / Ceilings	☐	☐	☐
Flooring	☐	☐	☐
Stairs	☐	☐	☐
Storage	☐	☐	☐
Living Room	☐	☐	☐
Family Room	☐	☐	☐
Dining Room	☐	☐	☐

	Good	Average	Poor
Master Bedroom	☐	☐	☐
Bedroom 2	☐	☐	☐
Bedroom 3	☐	☐	☐
Bedroom 4	☐	☐	☐
Master Bathroom	☐	☐	☐
Bathroom 2	☐	☐	☐
Bathroom 3	☐	☐	☐
Bonus / Game Room	☐	☐	☐

	Good	Average	Poor
Kitchen			
Cabinets	☐	☐	☐
Countertop	☐	☐	☐
Counter Space	☐	☐	☐
Flooring	☐	☐	☐
Oven / Stove	☐	☐	☐
Microwave	☐	☐	☐
Layout	☐	☐	☐
Light Fixtures	☐	☐	☐
Backsplash	☐	☐	☐
Pantry	☐	☐	☐
Appliances	☐	☐	☐
Island	☐	☐	☐

	Good	Average	Poor
Basement	☐	☐	☐
Garage	☐	☐	☐

COMMUNITY

	Good	Average	Poor
Immediate Neighborhood	☐	☐	☐
Close to Employment	☐	☐	☐
Close to Shopping	☐	☐	☐
Close to Transportation	☐	☐	☐
Close to Schools / Daycare	☐	☐	☐
Close to Places of Worship	☐	☐	☐
Near Recreational Facilities	☐	☐	☐
Close to Airport	☐	☐	☐
Near Police and Fire Department	☐	☐	☐

Address _____ Price _____

Bedrooms _____ Bathrooms _____ Sq.Ft. _____

Lot Size: _____ Year Built _____ School District _____

Annual Tax _____

EXTERIOR

	Good	Average	Poor
View/Yard/Landscaping	☐	☐	☐
Trees	☐	☐	☐
Lawn (Front)	☐	☐	☐
Lawn (Back)	☐	☐	☐
Fences (condition)	☐	☐	☐
Landscaping (condition)	☐	☐	☐
Irrigation / Sprinkler	☐	☐	☐
House Type	☐	☐	☐
Exterior Siding	☐	☐	☐
Deck / Patio / Porch	☐	☐	☐
Garage	☐	☐	☐
Window / Doors	☐	☐	☐
Roof / Gutters	☐	☐	☐
Fencing	☐	☐	☐

HOME SYSTEMS

	Good	Average	Poor
Electrical	☐	☐	☐
Air Conditioning / Fans	☐	☐	☐
Heating	☐	☐	☐
Security	☐	☐	☐
Plumbing	☐	☐	☐
Intercom	☐	☐	☐

FEATURES

	Good	Average	Poor
Home Warranty	☐	☐	☐
Energy Saving Features	☐	☐	☐

INTERIOR

	Good	Average	Poor
Walls / Trim / Ceilings	☐	☐	☐
Flooring	☐	☐	☐
Stairs	☐	☐	☐
Storage	☐	☐	☐
Living Room	☐	☐	☐
Family Room	☐	☐	☐
Dining Room	☐	☐	☐

	Good	Average	Poor
Master Bedroom	☐	☐	☐
Bedroom 2	☐	☐	☐
Bedroom 3	☐	☐	☐
Bedroom 4	☐	☐	☐
Master Bathroom	☐	☐	☐
Bathroom 2	☐	☐	☐
Bathroom 3	☐	☐	☐
Bonus / Game Room	☐	☐	☐

	Good	Average	Poor
Kitchen	☐	☐	☐
Cabinets	☐	☐	☐
Countertop	☐	☐	☐
Counter Space	☐	☐	☐
Flooring	☐	☐	☐
Oven / Stove	☐	☐	☐
Microwave	☐	☐	☐
Layout	☐	☐	☐
Light Fixtures	☐	☐	☐
Backsplash	☐	☐	☐
Pantry	☐	☐	☐
Appliances	☐	☐	☐
Island	☐	☐	☐

	Good	Average	Poor
Basement	☐	☐	☐
Garage	☐	☐	☐

COMMUNITY

	Good	Average	Poor
Immediate Neighborhood	☐	☐	☐
Close to Employment	☐	☐	☐
Close to Shopping	☐	☐	☐
Close to Transportation	☐	☐	☐
Close to Schools / Daycare	☐	☐	☐
Close to Places of Worship	☐	☐	☐
Near Recreational Facilities	☐	☐	☐
Close to Airport	☐	☐	☐
Near Police and Fire Department	☐	☐	☐

Address _____ Price _____

Bedrooms _____ Bathrooms _____ Sq.Ft. _____

Lot Size: _____ Year Built _____ School District _____

Annual Tax _____

EXTERIOR

	Good	Average	Poor
View/Yard/Landscaping	☐	☐	☐
Trees	☐	☐	☐
Lawn (Front)	☐	☐	☐
Lawn (Back)	☐	☐	☐
Fences (condition)	☐	☐	☐
Landscaping (condition)	☐	☐	☐
Irrigation / Sprinkler	☐	☐	☐
	☐	☐	☐
House Type	☐	☐	☐
Exterior Siding	☐	☐	☐
Deck / Patio / Porch	☐	☐	☐
Garage	☐	☐	☐
Window / Doors	☐	☐	☐
Roof / Gutters	☐	☐	☐
Fencing	☐	☐	☐

HOME SYSTEMS

	Good	Average	Poor
Electrical	☐	☐	☐
Air Conditioning / Fans	☐	☐	☐
Heating	☐	☐	☐
Security	☐	☐	☐
Plumbing	☐	☐	☐
Intercom	☐	☐	☐

FEATURES

	Good	Average	Poor
Home Warranty	☐	☐	☐
Energy Saving Features	☐	☐	☐

INTERIOR

	Good	Average	Poor
Walls / Trim / Ceilings	☐	☐	☐
Flooring	☐	☐	☐
Stairs	☐	☐	☐
Storage	☐	☐	☐
Living Room	☐	☐	☐
Family Room	☐	☐	☐
Dining Room	☐	☐	☐

	Good	Average	Poor
Master Bedroom	☐	☐	☐
Bedroom 2	☐	☐	☐
Bedroom 3	☐	☐	☐
Bedroom 4	☐	☐	☐
Master Bathroom	☐	☐	☐
Bathroom 2	☐	☐	☐
Bathroom 3	☐	☐	☐
Bonus / Game Room	☐	☐	☐

	Good	Average	Poor
Kitchen	☐	☐	☐
Cabinets	☐	☐	☐
Countertop	☐	☐	☐
Counter Space	☐	☐	☐
Flooring	☐	☐	☐
Oven / Stove	☐	☐	☐
Microwave	☐	☐	☐
Layout	☐	☐	☐
Light Fixtures	☐	☐	☐
Backsplash	☐	☐	☐
Pantry	☐	☐	☐
Appliances	☐	☐	☐
Island	☐	☐	☐

	Good	Average	Poor
Basement	☐	☐	☐
Garage	☐	☐	☐

COMMUNITY

	Good	Average	Poor
Immediate Neighborhood	☐	☐	☐
Close to Employment	☐	☐	☐
Close to Shopping	☐	☐	☐
Close to Transportation	☐	☐	☐
Close to Schools / Daycare	☐	☐	☐
Close to Places of Worship	☐	☐	☐
Near Recreational Facilities	☐	☐	☐
Close to Airport	☐	☐	☐
Near Police and Fire Department	☐	☐	☐

Address _____ Price _____

Bedrooms _____ Bathrooms _____ Sq.Ft. _____

Lot Size: _____ Year Built _____ School District _____

Annual Tax _____

EXTERIOR

	Good	Average	Poor
View/Yard/Landscaping	☐	☐	☐
Trees	☐	☐	☐
Lawn (Front)	☐	☐	☐
Lawn (Back)	☐	☐	☐
Fences (condition)	☐	☐	☐
Landscaping (condition)	☐	☐	☐
Irrigation / Sprinkler	☐	☐	☐
	☐	☐	☐
House Type	☐	☐	☐
Exterior Siding	☐	☐	☐
Deck / Patio / Porch	☐	☐	☐
Garage	☐	☐	☐
Window / Doors	☐	☐	☐
Roof / Gutters	☐	☐	☐
Fencing	☐	☐	☐

HOME SYSTEMS

	Good	Average	Poor
Electrical	☐	☐	☐
Air Conditioning / Fans	☐	☐	☐
Heating	☐	☐	☐
Security	☐	☐	☐
Plumbing	☐	☐	☐
Intercom	☐	☐	☐

FEATURES

	Good	Average	Poor
Home Warranty	☐	☐	☐
Energy Saving Features	☐	☐	☐

INTERIOR

	Good	Average	Poor
Walls / Trim / Ceilings	☐	☐	☐
Flooring	☐	☐	☐
Stairs	☐	☐	☐
Storage	☐	☐	☐
Living Room	☐	☐	☐
Family Room	☐	☐	☐
Dining Room	☐	☐	☐

	Good	Average	Poor
Master Bedroom	☐	☐	☐
Bedroom 2	☐	☐	☐
Bedroom 3	☐	☐	☐
Bedroom 4	☐	☐	☐
Master Bathroom	☐	☐	☐
Bathroom 2	☐	☐	☐
Bathroom 3	☐	☐	☐
Bonus / Game Room	☐	☐	☐

	Good	Average	Poor
Kitchen			
Cabinets	☐	☐	☐
Countertop	☐	☐	☐
Counter Space	☐	☐	☐
Flooring	☐	☐	☐
Oven / Stove	☐	☐	☐
Microwave	☐	☐	☐
Layout	☐	☐	☐
Light Fixtures	☐	☐	☐
Backsplash	☐	☐	☐
Pantry	☐	☐	☐
Appliances	☐	☐	☐
Island	☐	☐	☐

	Good	Average	Poor
Basement	☐	☐	☐
Garage	☐	☐	☐

COMMUNITY

	Good	Average	Poor
Immediate Neighborhood	☐	☐	☐
Close to Employment	☐	☐	☐
Close to Shopping	☐	☐	☐
Close to Transportation	☐	☐	☐
Close to Schools / Daycare	☐	☐	☐
Close to Places of Worship	☐	☐	☐
Near Recreational Facilities	☐	☐	☐
Close to Airport	☐	☐	☐
Near Police and Fire Department	☐	☐	☐

Address _____ Price _____

Bedrooms _____ Bathrooms _____ Sq.Ft. _____

Lot Size: _____ Year Built _____ School District _____

Annual Tax _____

EXTERIOR

	Good	Average	Poor
View/Yard/Landscaping	☐	☐	☐
Trees	☐	☐	☐
Lawn (Front)	☐	☐	☐
Lawn (Back)	☐	☐	☐
Fences (condition)	☐	☐	☐
Landscaping (condition)	☐	☐	☐
Irrigation / Sprinkler	☐	☐	☐
	☐	☐	☐
House Type	☐	☐	☐
Exterior Siding	☐	☐	☐
Deck / Patio / Porch	☐	☐	☐
Garage	☐	☐	☐
Window / Doors	☐	☐	☐
Roof / Gutters	☐	☐	☐
Fencing	☐	☐	☐

HOME SYSTEMS

	Good	Average	Poor
Electrical	☐	☐	☐
Air Conditioning / Fans	☐	☐	☐
Heating	☐	☐	☐
Security	☐	☐	☐
Plumbing	☐	☐	☐
Intercom	☐	☐	☐

FEATURES

	Good	Average	Poor
Home Warranty	☐	☐	☐
Energy Saving Features	☐	☐	☐

INTERIOR

	Good	Average	Poor
Walls / Trim / Ceilings	☐	☐	☐
Flooring	☐	☐	☐
Stairs	☐	☐	☐
Storage	☐	☐	☐
Living Room	☐	☐	☐
Family Room	☐	☐	☐
Dining Room	☐	☐	☐

	Good	Average	Poor
Master Bedroom	☐	☐	☐
Bedroom 2	☐	☐	☐
Bedroom 3	☐	☐	☐
Bedroom 4	☐	☐	☐
Master Bathroom	☐	☐	☐
Bathroom 2	☐	☐	☐
Bathroom 3	☐	☐	☐
Bonus / Game Room	☐	☐	☐

	Good	Average	Poor
Kitchen	☐	☐	☐
Cabinets	☐	☐	☐
Countertop	☐	☐	☐
Counter Space	☐	☐	☐
Flooring	☐	☐	☐
Oven / Stove	☐	☐	☐
Microwave	☐	☐	☐
Layout	☐	☐	☐
Light Fixtures	☐	☐	☐
Backsplash	☐	☐	☐
Pantry	☐	☐	☐
Appliances	☐	☐	☐
Island	☐	☐	☐

	Good	Average	Poor
Basement	☐	☐	☐
Garage	☐	☐	☐

COMMUNITY

	Good	Average	Poor
Immediate Neighborhood	☐	☐	☐
Close to Employment	☐	☐	☐
Close to Shopping	☐	☐	☐
Close to Transportation	☐	☐	☐
Close to Schools / Daycare	☐	☐	☐
Close to Places of Worship	☐	☐	☐
Near Recreational Facilities	☐	☐	☐
Close to Airport	☐	☐	☐
Near Police and Fire Department	☐	☐	☐

Address _____ Price _____

Bedrooms _____ Bathrooms _____ Sq.Ft. _____

Lot Size: _____ Year Built _____ School District _____

Annual Tax _____

EXTERIOR

	Good	Average	Poor
View/Yard/Landscaping	☐	☐	☐
Trees	☐	☐	☐
Lawn (Front)	☐	☐	☐
Lawn (Back)	☐	☐	☐
Fences (condition)	☐	☐	☐
Landscaping (condition)	☐	☐	☐
Irrigation / Sprinkler	☐	☐	☐
	☐	☐	☐
House Type	☐	☐	☐
Exterior Siding	☐	☐	☐
Deck / Patio / Porch	☐	☐	☐
Garage	☐	☐	☐
Window / Doors	☐	☐	☐
Roof / Gutters	☐	☐	☐
Fencing	☐	☐	☐

HOME SYSTEMS

	Good	Average	Poor
Electrical	☐	☐	☐
Air Conditioning / Fans	☐	☐	☐
Heating	☐	☐	☐
Security	☐	☐	☐
Plumbing	☐	☐	☐
Intercom	☐	☐	☐

FEATURES

	Good	Average	Poor
Home Warranty	☐	☐	☐
Energy Saving Features	☐	☐	☐

INTERIOR

	Good	Average	Poor
Walls / Trim / Ceilings	☐	☐	☐
Flooring	☐	☐	☐
Stairs	☐	☐	☐
Storage	☐	☐	☐
Living Room	☐	☐	☐
Family Room	☐	☐	☐
Dining Room	☐	☐	☐

	Good	Average	Poor
Master Bedroom	☐	☐	☐
Bedroom 2	☐	☐	☐
Bedroom 3	☐	☐	☐
Bedroom 4	☐	☐	☐
Master Bathroom	☐	☐	☐
Bathroom 2	☐	☐	☐
Bathroom 3	☐	☐	☐
Bonus / Game Room	☐	☐	☐

	Good	Average	Poor
Kitchen	☐	☐	☐
Cabinets	☐	☐	☐
Countertop	☐	☐	☐
Counter Space	☐	☐	☐
Flooring	☐	☐	☐
Oven / Stove	☐	☐	☐
Microwave	☐	☐	☐
Layout	☐	☐	☐
Light Fixtures	☐	☐	☐
Backsplash	☐	☐	☐
Pantry	☐	☐	☐
Appliances	☐	☐	☐
Island	☐	☐	☐

	Good	Average	Poor
Basement	☐	☐	☐
Garage	☐	☐	☐

COMMUNITY

	Good	Average	Poor
Immediate Neighborhood	☐	☐	☐
Close to Employment	☐	☐	☐
Close to Shopping	☐	☐	☐
Close to Transportation	☐	☐	☐
Close to Schools / Daycare	☐	☐	☐
Close to Places of Worship	☐	☐	☐
Near Recreational Facilities	☐	☐	☐
Close to Airport	☐	☐	☐
Near Police and Fire Department	☐	☐	☐

Address _____   Price _____

Bedrooms _____   Bathrooms _____   Sq.Ft. _____

Lot Size: _____   Year Built _____   School District _____

Annual Tax _____

EXTERIOR

	Good	Average	Poor
View/Yard/Landscaping	☐	☐	☐
Trees	☐	☐	☐
Lawn (Front)	☐	☐	☐
Lawn (Back)	☐	☐	☐
Fences (condition)	☐	☐	☐
Landscaping (condition)	☐	☐	☐
Irrigation / Sprinkler	☐	☐	☐
House Type	☐	☐	☐
Exterior Siding	☐	☐	☐
Deck / Patio / Porch	☐	☐	☐
Garage	☐	☐	☐
Window / Doors	☐	☐	☐
Roof / Gutters	☐	☐	☐
Fencing	☐	☐	☐

HOME SYSTEMS

	Good	Average	Poor
Electrical	☐	☐	☐
Air Conditioning / Fans	☐	☐	☐
Heating	☐	☐	☐
Security	☐	☐	☐
Plumbing	☐	☐	☐
Intercom	☐	☐	☐

FEATURES

	Good	Average	Poor
Home Warranty	☐	☐	☐
Energy Saving Features	☐	☐	☐

INTERIOR

	Good	Average	Poor
Walls / Trim / Ceilings	☐	☐	☐
Flooring	☐	☐	☐
Stairs	☐	☐	☐
Storage	☐	☐	☐
Living Room	☐	☐	☐
Family Room	☐	☐	☐
Dining Room	☐	☐	☐

	Good	Average	Poor
Master Bedroom	☐	☐	☐
Bedroom 2	☐	☐	☐
Bedroom 3	☐	☐	☐
Bedroom 4	☐	☐	☐
Master Bathroom	☐	☐	☐
Bathroom 2	☐	☐	☐
Bathroom 3	☐	☐	☐
Bonus / Game Room	☐	☐	☐

Kitchen

	Good	Average	Poor
Cabinets	☐	☐	☐
Countertop	☐	☐	☐
Counter Space	☐	☐	☐
Flooring	☐	☐	☐
Oven / Stove	☐	☐	☐
Microwave	☐	☐	☐
Layout	☐	☐	☐
Light Fixtures	☐	☐	☐
Backsplash	☐	☐	☐
Pantry	☐	☐	☐
Appliances	☐	☐	☐
Island	☐	☐	☐

	Good	Average	Poor
Basement	☐	☐	☐
Garage	☐	☐	☐

COMMUNITY

	Good	Average	Poor
Immediate Neighborhood	☐	☐	☐
Close to Employment	☐	☐	☐
Close to Shopping	☐	☐	☐
Close to Transportation	☐	☐	☐
Close to Schools / Daycare	☐	☐	☐
Close to Places of Worship	☐	☐	☐
Near Recreational Facilities	☐	☐	☐
Close to Airport	☐	☐	☐
Near Police and Fire Department	☐	☐	☐

Address _____ Price _____

Bedrooms _____ Bathrooms _____ Sq.Ft. _____

Lot Size: _____ Year Built _____ School District _____

Annual Tax _____

EXTERIOR

	Good	Average	Poor
View/Yard/Landscaping	☐	☐	☐
Trees	☐	☐	☐
Lawn (Front)	☐	☐	☐
Lawn (Back)	☐	☐	☐
Fences (condition)	☐	☐	☐
Landscaping (condition)	☐	☐	☐
Irrigation / Sprinkler	☐	☐	☐
	☐	☐	☐
House Type	☐	☐	☐
Exterior Siding	☐	☐	☐
Deck / Patio / Porch	☐	☐	☐
Garage	☐	☐	☐
Window / Doors	☐	☐	☐
Roof / Gutters	☐	☐	☐
Fencing	☐	☐	☐

HOME SYSTEMS

	Good	Average	Poor
Electrical	☐	☐	☐
Air Conditioning / Fans	☐	☐	☐
Heating	☐	☐	☐
Security	☐	☐	☐
Plumbing	☐	☐	☐
Intercom	☐	☐	☐

FEATURES

	Good	Average	Poor
Home Warranty	☐	☐	☐
Energy Saving Features	☐	☐	☐

INTERIOR

	Good	Average	Poor
Walls / Trim / Ceilings	☐	☐	☐
Flooring	☐	☐	☐
Stairs	☐	☐	☐
Storage	☐	☐	☐
Living Room	☐	☐	☐
Family Room	☐	☐	☐
Dining Room	☐	☐	☐

	Good	Average	Poor
Master Bedroom	☐	☐	☐
Bedroom 2	☐	☐	☐
Bedroom 3	☐	☐	☐
Bedroom 4	☐	☐	☐
Master Bathroom	☐	☐	☐
Bathroom 2	☐	☐	☐
Bathroom 3	☐	☐	☐
Bonus / Game Room	☐	☐	☐

	Good	Average	Poor
Kitchen	☐	☐	
Cabinets	☐	☐	☐
Countertop	☐	☐	☐
Counter Space	☐	☐	☐
Flooring	☐	☐	☐
Oven / Stove	☐	☐	☐
Microwave	☐	☐	☐
Layout	☐	☐	☐
Light Fixtures	☐	☐	☐
Backsplash	☐	☐	☐
Pantry	☐	☐	☐
Appliances	☐	☐	☐
Island	☐	☐	☐

	Good	Average	Poor
Basement	☐	☐	☐
Garage	☐	☐	☐

COMMUNITY

	Good	Average	Poor
Immediate Neighborhood	☐	☐	☐
Close to Employment	☐	☐	☐
Close to Shopping	☐	☐	☐
Close to Transportation	☐	☐	☐
Close to Schools / Daycare	☐	☐	☐
Close to Places of Worship	☐	☐	☐
Near Recreational Facilities	☐	☐	☐
Close to Airport	☐	☐	☐
Near Police and Fire Department	☐	☐	☐

Address _____ Price _____

Bedrooms _____ Bathrooms _____ Sq.Ft. _____

Lot Size: _____ Year Built _____ School District _____

Annual Tax _____

EXTERIOR

	Good	Average	Poor
View/Yard/Landscaping	☐	☐	☐
Trees	☐	☐	☐
Lawn (Front)	☐	☐	☐
Lawn (Back)	☐	☐	☐
Fences (condition)	☐	☐	☐
Landscaping (condition)	☐	☐	☐
Irrigation / Sprinkler	☐	☐	☐
	☐	☐	☐
House Type	☐	☐	☐
Exterior Siding	☐	☐	☐
Deck / Patio / Porch	☐	☐	☐
Garage	☐	☐	☐
Window / Doors	☐	☐	☐
Roof / Gutters	☐	☐	☐
Fencing	☐	☐	☐

HOME SYSTEMS

	Good	Average	Poor
Electrical	☐	☐	☐
Air Conditioning / Fans	☐	☐	☐
Heating	☐	☐	☐
Security	☐	☐	☐
Plumbing	☐	☐	☐
Intercom	☐	☐	☐

FEATURES

	Good	Average	Poor
Home Warranty	☐	☐	☐
Energy Saving Features	☐	☐	☐

INTERIOR

	Good	Average	Poor
Walls / Trim / Ceilings	☐	☐	☐
Flooring	☐	☐	☐
Stairs	☐	☐	☐
Storage	☐	☐	☐
Living Room	☐	☐	☐
Family Room	☐	☐	☐
Dining Room	☐	☐	☐

	Good	Average	Poor
Master Bedroom	☐	☐	☐
Bedroom 2	☐	☐	☐
Bedroom 3	☐	☐	☐
Bedroom 4	☐	☐	☐
Master Bathroom	☐	☐	☐
Bathroom 2	☐	☐	☐
Bathroom 3	☐	☐	☐
Bonus / Game Room	☐	☐	☐

	Good	Average	Poor
Kitchen			
Cabinets	☐	☐	☐
Countertop	☐	☐	☐
Counter Space	☐	☐	☐
Flooring	☐	☐	☐
Oven / Stove	☐	☐	☐
Microwave	☐	☐	☐
Layout	☐	☐	☐
Light Fixtures	☐	☐	☐
Backsplash	☐	☐	☐
Pantry	☐	☐	☐
Appliances	☐	☐	☐
Island	☐	☐	☐

	Good	Average	Poor
Basement	☐	☐	☐
Garage	☐	☐	☐

COMMUNITY

	Good	Average	Poor
Immediate Neighborhood	☐	☐	☐
Close to Employment	☐	☐	☐
Close to Shopping	☐	☐	☐
Close to Transportation	☐	☐	☐
Close to Schools / Daycare	☐	☐	☐
Close to Places of Worship	☐	☐	☐
Near Recreational Facilities	☐	☐	☐
Close to Airport	☐	☐	☐
Near Police and Fire Department	☐	☐	☐

Address _____ Price _____

Bedrooms _____ Bathrooms _____ Sq.Ft. _____

Lot Size: _____ Year Built _____ School District _____

Annual Tax _____

EXTERIOR

	Good	Average	Poor
View/Yard/Landscaping	☐	☐	☐
Trees	☐	☐	☐
Lawn (Front)	☐	☐	☐
Lawn (Back)	☐	☐	☐
Fences (condition)	☐	☐	☐
Landscaping (condition)	☐	☐	☐
Irrigation / Sprinkler	☐	☐	☐
	☐	☐	☐
House Type	☐	☐	☐
Exterior Siding	☐	☐	☐
Deck / Patio / Porch	☐	☐	☐
Garage	☐	☐	☐
Window / Doors	☐	☐	☐
Roof / Gutters	☐	☐	☐
Fencing	☐	☐	☐

HOME SYSTEMS

	Good	Average	Poor
Electrical	☐	☐	☐
Air Conditioning / Fans	☐	☐	☐
Heating	☐	☐	☐
Security	☐	☐	☐
Plumbing	☐	☐	☐
Intercom	☐	☐	☐

FEATURES

	Good	Average	Poor
Home Warranty	☐	☐	☐
Energy Saving Features	☐	☐	☐

INTERIOR

	Good	Average	Poor
Walls / Trim / Ceilings	☐	☐	☐
Flooring	☐	☐	☐
Stairs	☐	☐	☐
Storage	☐	☐	☐
Living Room	☐	☐	☐
Family Room	☐	☐	☐
Dining Room	☐	☐	☐

	Good	Average	Poor
Master Bedroom	☐	☐	☐
Bedroom 2	☐	☐	☐
Bedroom 3	☐	☐	☐
Bedroom 4	☐	☐	☐
Master Bathroom	☐	☐	☐
Bathroom 2	☐	☐	☐
Bathroom 3	☐	☐	☐
Bonus / Game Room	☐	☐	☐

	Good	Average	Poor
Kitchen			
Cabinets	☐	☐	☐
Countertop	☐	☐	☐
Counter Space	☐	☐	☐
Flooring	☐	☐	☐
Oven / Stove	☐	☐	☐
Microwave	☐	☐	☐
Layout	☐	☐	☐
Light Fixtures	☐	☐	☐
Backsplash	☐	☐	☐
Pantry	☐	☐	☐
Appliances	☐	☐	☐
Island	☐	☐	☐

	Good	Average	Poor
Basement	☐	☐	☐
Garage	☐	☐	☐

COMMUNITY

	Good	Average	Poor
Immediate Neighborhood	☐	☐	☐
Close to Employment	☐	☐	☐
Close to Shopping	☐	☐	☐
Close to Transportation	☐	☐	☐
Close to Schools / Daycare	☐	☐	☐
Close to Places of Worship	☐	☐	☐
Near Recreational Facilities	☐	☐	☐
Close to Airport	☐	☐	☐
Near Police and Fire Department	☐	☐	☐

Address _____ Price _____

Bedrooms _____ Bathrooms _____ Sq.Ft. _____

Lot Size: _____ Year Built _____ School District _____

Annual Tax _____

EXTERIOR

	Good	Average	Poor
View/Yard/Landscaping	☐	☐	☐
Trees	☐	☐	☐
Lawn (Front)	☐	☐	☐
Lawn (Back)	☐	☐	☐
Fences (condition)	☐	☐	☐
Landscaping (condition)	☐	☐	☐
Irrigation / Sprinkler	☐	☐	☐
House Type	☐	☐	☐
Exterior Siding	☐	☐	☐
Deck / Patio / Porch	☐	☐	☐
Garage	☐	☐	☐
Window / Doors	☐	☐	☐
Roof / Gutters	☐	☐	☐
Fencing	☐	☐	☐

HOME SYSTEMS

	Good	Average	Poor
Electrical	☐	☐	☐
Air Conditioning / Fans	☐	☐	☐
Heating	☐	☐	☐
Security	☐	☐	☐
Plumbing	☐	☐	☐
Intercom	☐	☐	☐

FEATURES

	Good	Average	Poor
Home Warranty	☐	☐	☐
Energy Saving Features	☐	☐	☐

INTERIOR

	Good	Average	Poor
Walls / Trim / Ceilings	☐	☐	☐
Flooring	☐	☐	☐
Stairs	☐	☐	☐
Storage	☐	☐	☐
Living Room	☐	☐	☐
Family Room	☐	☐	☐
Dining Room	☐	☐	☐

	Good	Average	Poor
Master Bedroom	☐	☐	☐
Bedroom 2	☐	☐	☐
Bedroom 3	☐	☐	☐
Bedroom 4	☐	☐	☐
Master Bathroom	☐	☐	☐
Bathroom 2	☐	☐	☐
Bathroom 3	☐	☐	☐
Bonus / Game Room	☐	☐	☐

	Good	Average	Poor
Kitchen			
Cabinets	☐	☐	☐
Countertop	☐	☐	☐
Counter Space	☐	☐	☐
Flooring	☐	☐	☐
Oven / Stove	☐	☐	☐
Microwave	☐	☐	☐
Layout	☐	☐	☐
Light Fixtures	☐	☐	☐
Backsplash	☐	☐	☐
Pantry	☐	☐	☐
Appliances	☐	☐	☐
Island	☐	☐	☐

	Good	Average	Poor
Basement	☐	☐	☐
Garage	☐	☐	☐

COMMUNITY

	Good	Average	Poor
Immediate Neighborhood	☐	☐	☐
Close to Employment	☐	☐	☐
Close to Shopping	☐	☐	☐
Close to Transportation	☐	☐	☐
Close to Schools / Daycare	☐	☐	☐
Close to Places of Worship	☐	☐	☐
Near Recreational Facilities	☐	☐	☐
Close to Airport	☐	☐	☐
Near Police and Fire Department	☐	☐	☐

Address _____ Price _____

Bedrooms _____ Bathrooms _____ Sq.Ft. _____

Lot Size: _____ Year Built _____ School District _____

Annual Tax _____

EXTERIOR

	Good	Average	Poor
View/Yard/Landscaping	☐	☐	☐
Trees	☐	☐	☐
Lawn (Front)	☐	☐	☐
Lawn (Back)	☐	☐	☐
Fences (condition)	☐	☐	☐
Landscaping (condition)	☐	☐	☐
Irrigation / Sprinkler	☐	☐	☐
	☐	☐	☐
House Type	☐	☐	☐
Exterior Siding	☐	☐	☐
Deck / Patio / Porch	☐	☐	☐
Garage	☐	☐	☐
Window / Doors	☐	☐	☐
Roof / Gutters	☐	☐	☐
Fencing	☐	☐	☐

HOME SYSTEMS

	Good	Average	Poor
Electrical	☐	☐	☐
Air Conditioning / Fans	☐	☐	☐
Heating	☐	☐	☐
Security	☐	☐	☐
Plumbing	☐	☐	☐
Intercom	☐	☐	☐

FEATURES

	Good	Average	Poor
Home Warranty	☐	☐	☐
Energy Saving Features	☐	☐	☐

INTERIOR

	Good	Average	Poor
Walls / Trim / Ceilings	☐	☐	☐
Flooring	☐	☐	☐
Stairs	☐	☐	☐
Storage	☐	☐	☐
Living Room	☐	☐	☐
Family Room	☐	☐	☐
Dining Room	☐	☐	☐

	Good	Average	Poor
Master Bedroom	☐	☐	☐
Bedroom 2	☐	☐	☐
Bedroom 3	☐	☐	☐
Bedroom 4	☐	☐	☐
Master Bathroom	☐	☐	☐
Bathroom 2	☐	☐	☐
Bathroom 3	☐	☐	☐
Bonus / Game Room	☐	☐	☐

	Good	Average	Poor
Kitchen	☐	☐	☐
Cabinets	☐	☐	☐
Countertop	☐	☐	☐
Counter Space	☐	☐	☐
Flooring	☐	☐	☐
Oven / Stove	☐	☐	☐
Microwave	☐	☐	☐
Layout	☐	☐	☐
Light Fixtures	☐	☐	☐
Backsplash	☐	☐	☐
Pantry	☐	☐	☐
Appliances	☐	☐	☐
Island	☐	☐	☐

	Good	Average	Poor
Basement	☐	☐	☐
Garage	☐	☐	☐

COMMUNITY

	Good	Average	Poor
Immediate Neighborhood	☐	☐	☐
Close to Employment	☐	☐	☐
Close to Shopping	☐	☐	☐
Close to Transportation	☐	☐	☐
Close to Schools / Daycare	☐	☐	☐
Close to Places of Worship	☐	☐	☐
Near Recreational Facilities	☐	☐	☐
Close to Airport	☐	☐	☐
Near Police and Fire Department	☐	☐	☐

Address _____ Price _____

Bedrooms _____ Bathrooms _____ Sq.Ft. _____

Lot Size: _____ Year Built _____ School District _____

Annual Tax _____

EXTERIOR

	Good	Average	Poor
View/Yard/Landscaping	☐	☐	☐
Trees	☐	☐	☐
Lawn (Front)	☐	☐	☐
Lawn (Back)	☐	☐	☐
Fences (condition)	☐	☐	☐
Landscaping (condition)	☐	☐	☐
Irrigation / Sprinkler	☐	☐	☐
	☐	☐	☐
House Type	☐	☐	☐
Exterior Siding	☐	☐	☐
Deck / Patio / Porch	☐	☐	☐
Garage	☐	☐	☐
Window / Doors	☐	☐	☐
Roof / Gutters	☐	☐	☐
Fencing	☐	☐	☐

HOME SYSTEMS

	Good	Average	Poor
Electrical	☐	☐	☐
Air Conditioning / Fans	☐	☐	☐
Heating	☐	☐	☐
Security	☐	☐	☐
Plumbing	☐	☐	☐
Intercom	☐	☐	☐

FEATURES

	Good	Average	Poor
Home Warranty	☐	☐	☐
Energy Saving Features	☐	☐	☐

INTERIOR

	Good	Average	Poor
Walls / Trim / Ceilings	☐	☐	☐
Flooring	☐	☐	☐
Stairs	☐	☐	☐
Storage	☐	☐	☐
Living Room	☐	☐	☐
Family Room	☐	☐	☐
Dining Room	☐	☐	☐

	Good	Average	Poor
Master Bedroom	☐	☐	☐
Bedroom 2	☐	☐	☐
Bedroom 3	☐	☐	☐
Bedroom 4	☐	☐	☐
Master Bathroom	☐	☐	☐
Bathroom 2	☐	☐	☐
Bathroom 3	☐	☐	☐
Bonus / Game Room	☐	☐	☐

	Good	Average	Poor
Kitchen	☐	☐	☐
Cabinets	☐	☐	☐
Countertop	☐	☐	☐
Counter Space	☐	☐	☐
Flooring	☐	☐	☐
Oven / Stove	☐	☐	☐
Microwave	☐	☐	☐
Layout	☐	☐	☐
Light Fixtures	☐	☐	☐
Backsplash	☐	☐	☐
Pantry	☐	☐	☐
Appliances	☐	☐	☐
Island	☐	☐	☐

	Good	Average	Poor
Basement	☐	☐	☐
Garage	☐	☐	☐

COMMUNITY

	Good	Average	Poor
Immediate Neighborhood	☐	☐	☐
Close to Employment	☐	☐	☐
Close to Shopping	☐	☐	☐
Close to Transportation	☐	☐	☐
Close to Schools / Daycare	☐	☐	☐
Close to Places of Worship	☐	☐	☐
Near Recreational Facilities	☐	☐	☐
Close to Airport	☐	☐	☐
Near Police and Fire Department	☐	☐	☐

Address _____ Price _____

Bedrooms _____ Bathrooms _____ Sq.Ft. _____

Lot Size: _____ Year Built _____ School District _____

Annual Tax _____

EXTERIOR

	Good	Average	Poor
View/Yard/Landscaping	☐	☐	☐
Trees	☐	☐	☐
Lawn (Front)	☐	☐	☐
Lawn (Back)	☐	☐	☐
Fences (condition)	☐	☐	☐
Landscaping (condition)	☐	☐	☐
Irrigation / Sprinkler	☐	☐	☐
	☐	☐	☐
House Type	☐	☐	☐
Exterior Siding	☐	☐	☐
Deck / Patio / Porch	☐	☐	☐
Garage	☐	☐	☐
Window / Doors	☐	☐	☐
Roof / Gutters	☐	☐	☐
Fencing	☐	☐	☐

HOME SYSTEMS

	Good	Average	Poor
Electrical	☐	☐	☐
Air Conditioning / Fans	☐	☐	☐
Heating	☐	☐	☐
Security	☐	☐	☐
Plumbing	☐	☐	☐
Intercom	☐	☐	☐

FEATURES

	Good	Average	Poor
Home Warranty	☐	☐	☐
Energy Saving Features	☐	☐	☐

INTERIOR

	Good	Average	Poor
Walls / Trim / Ceilings	☐	☐	☐
Flooring	☐	☐	☐
Stairs	☐	☐	☐
Storage	☐	☐	☐
Living Room	☐	☐	☐
Family Room	☐	☐	☐
Dining Room	☐	☐	☐

	Good	Average	Poor
Master Bedroom	☐	☐	☐
Bedroom 2	☐	☐	☐
Bedroom 3	☐	☐	☐
Bedroom 4	☐	☐	☐
Master Bathroom	☐	☐	☐
Bathroom 2	☐	☐	☐
Bathroom 3	☐	☐	☐
Bonus / Game Room	☐	☐	☐

	Good	Average	Poor
Kitchen	☐	☐	☐
Cabinets	☐	☐	☐
Countertop	☐	☐	☐
Counter Space	☐	☐	☐
Flooring	☐	☐	☐
Oven / Stove	☐	☐	☐
Microwave	☐	☐	☐
Layout	☐	☐	☐
Light Fixtures	☐	☐	☐
Backsplash	☐	☐	☐
Pantry	☐	☐	☐
Appliances	☐	☐	☐
Island	☐	☐	☐

	Good	Average	Poor
Basement	☐	☐	☐
Garage	☐	☐	☐

COMMUNITY

	Good	Average	Poor
Immediate Neighborhood	☐	☐	☐
Close to Employment	☐	☐	☐
Close to Shopping	☐	☐	☐
Close to Transportation	☐	☐	☐
Close to Schools / Daycare	☐	☐	☐
Close to Places of Worship	☐	☐	☐
Near Recreational Facilities	☐	☐	☐
Close to Airport	☐	☐	☐
Near Police and Fire Department	☐	☐	☐

Address _____   Price _____

Bedrooms _____   Bathrooms _____   Sq.Ft. _____

Lot Size: _____   Year Built _____   School District _____

Annual Tax _____

EXTERIOR

	Good	Average	Poor
View/Yard/Landscaping	☐	☐	☐
Trees	☐	☐	☐
Lawn (Front)	☐	☐	☐
Lawn (Back)	☐	☐	☐
Fences (condition)	☐	☐	☐
Landscaping (condition)	☐	☐	☐
Irrigation / Sprinkler	☐	☐	☐
	☐	☐	☐
House Type	☐	☐	☐
Exterior Siding	☐	☐	☐
Deck / Patio / Porch	☐	☐	☐
Garage	☐	☐	☐
Window / Doors	☐	☐	☐
Roof / Gutters	☐	☐	☐
Fencing	☐	☐	☐

HOME SYSTEMS

	Good	Average	Poor
Electrical	☐	☐	☐
Air Conditioning / Fans	☐	☐	☐
Heating	☐	☐	☐
Security	☐	☐	☐
Plumbing	☐	☐	☐
Intercom	☐	☐	☐

FEATURES

	Good	Average	Poor
Home Warranty	☐	☐	☐
Energy Saving Features	☐	☐	☐

INTERIOR

	Good	Average	Poor
Walls / Trim / Ceilings	☐	☐	☐
Flooring	☐	☐	☐
Stairs	☐	☐	☐
Storage	☐	☐	☐
Living Room	☐	☐	☐
Family Room	☐	☐	☐
Dining Room	☐	☐	☐

	Good	Average	Poor
Master Bedroom	☐	☐	☐
Bedroom 2	☐	☐	☐
Bedroom 3	☐	☐	☐
Bedroom 4	☐	☐	☐
Master Bathroom	☐	☐	☐
Bathroom 2	☐	☐	☐
Bathroom 3	☐	☐	☐
Bonus / Game Room	☐	☐	☐

	Good	Average	Poor
Kitchen	☐	☐	☐
Cabinets	☐	☐	☐
Countertop	☐	☐	☐
Counter Space	☐	☐	☐
Flooring	☐	☐	☐
Oven / Stove	☐	☐	☐
Microwave	☐	☐	☐
Layout	☐	☐	☐
Light Fixtures	☐	☐	☐
Backsplash	☐	☐	☐
Pantry	☐	☐	☐
Appliances	☐	☐	☐
Island	☐	☐	☐

	Good	Average	Poor
Basement	☐	☐	☐
Garage	☐	☐	☐

COMMUNITY

	Good	Average	Poor
Immediate Neighborhood	☐	☐	☐
Close to Employment	☐	☐	☐
Close to Shopping	☐	☐	☐
Close to Transportation	☐	☐	☐
Close to Schools / Daycare	☐	☐	☐
Close to Places of Worship	☐	☐	☐
Near Recreational Facilities	☐	☐	☐
Close to Airport	☐	☐	☐
Near Police and Fire Department	☐	☐	☐

Address _____ Price _____

Bedrooms _____ Bathrooms _____ Sq.Ft. _____

Lot Size: _____ Year Built _____ School District _____

Annual Tax _____

EXTERIOR

	Good	Average	Poor
View/Yard/Landscaping	☐	☐	☐
Trees	☐	☐	☐
Lawn (Front)	☐	☐	☐
Lawn (Back)	☐	☐	☐
Fences (condition)	☐	☐	☐
Landscaping (condition)	☐	☐	☐
Irrigation / Sprinkler	☐	☐	☐
	☐	☐	☐
House Type	☐	☐	☐
Exterior Siding	☐	☐	☐
Deck / Patio / Porch	☐	☐	☐
Garage	☐	☐	☐
Window / Doors	☐	☐	☐
Roof / Gutters	☐	☐	☐
Fencing	☐	☐	☐

HOME SYSTEMS

	Good	Average	Poor
Electrical	☐	☐	☐
Air Conditioning / Fans	☐	☐	☐
Heating	☐	☐	☐
Security	☐	☐	☐
Plumbing	☐	☐	☐
Intercom	☐	☐	☐

FEATURES

	Good	Average	Poor
Home Warranty	☐	☐	☐
Energy Saving Features	☐	☐	☐

INTERIOR

	Good	Average	Poor
Walls / Trim / Ceilings	☐	☐	☐
Flooring	☐	☐	☐
Stairs	☐	☐	☐
Storage	☐	☐	☐
Living Room	☐	☐	☐
Family Room	☐	☐	☐
Dining Room	☐	☐	☐

	Good	Average	Poor
Master Bedroom	☐	☐	☐
Bedroom 2	☐	☐	☐
Bedroom 3	☐	☐	☐
Bedroom 4	☐	☐	☐
Master Bathroom	☐	☐	☐
Bathroom 2	☐	☐	☐
Bathroom 3	☐	☐	☐
Bonus / Game Room	☐	☐	☐

	Good	Average	Poor
Kitchen	☐	☐	☐
Cabinets	☐	☐	☐
Countertop	☐	☐	☐
Counter Space	☐	☐	☐
Flooring	☐	☐	☐
Oven / Stove	☐	☐	☐
Microwave	☐	☐	☐
Layout	☐	☐	☐
Light Fixtures	☐	☐	☐
Backsplash	☐	☐	☐
Pantry	☐	☐	☐
Appliances	☐	☐	☐
Island	☐	☐	☐

	Good	Average	Poor
Basement	☐	☐	☐
Garage	☐	☐	☐

COMMUNITY

	Good	Average	Poor
Immediate Neighborhood	☐	☐	☐
Close to Employment	☐	☐	☐
Close to Shopping	☐	☐	☐
Close to Transportation	☐	☐	☐
Close to Schools / Daycare	☐	☐	☐
Close to Places of Worship	☐	☐	☐
Near Recreational Facilities	☐	☐	☐
Close to Airport	☐	☐	☐
Near Police and Fire Department	☐	☐	☐

Address _____ Price _____

Bedrooms _____ Bathrooms _____ Sq.Ft. _____

Lot Size: _____ Year Built _____ School District _____

Annual Tax _____

EXTERIOR

	Good	Average	Poor
View/Yard/Landscaping	☐	☐	☐
Trees	☐	☐	☐
Lawn (Front)	☐	☐	☐
Lawn (Back)	☐	☐	☐
Fences (condition)	☐	☐	☐
Landscaping (condition)	☐	☐	☐
Irrigation / Sprinkler	☐	☐	☐
House Type	☐	☐	☐
Exterior Siding	☐	☐	☐
Deck / Patio / Porch	☐	☐	☐
Garage	☐	☐	☐
Window / Doors	☐	☐	☐
Roof / Gutters	☐	☐	☐
Fencing	☐	☐	☐

HOME SYSTEMS

	Good	Average	Poor
Electrical	☐	☐	☐
Air Conditioning / Fans	☐	☐	☐
Heating	☐	☐	☐
Security	☐	☐	☐
Plumbing	☐	☐	☐
Intercom	☐	☐	☐

FEATURES

	Good	Average	Poor
Home Warranty	☐	☐	☐
Energy Saving Features	☐	☐	☐

INTERIOR

	Good	Average	Poor
Walls / Trim / Ceilings	☐	☐	☐
Flooring	☐	☐	☐
Stairs	☐	☐	☐
Storage	☐	☐	☐
Living Room	☐	☐	☐
Family Room	☐	☐	☐
Dining Room	☐	☐	☐

	Good	Average	Poor
Master Bedroom	☐	☐	☐
Bedroom 2	☐	☐	☐
Bedroom 3	☐	☐	☐
Bedroom 4	☐	☐	☐
Master Bathroom	☐	☐	☐
Bathroom 2	☐	☐	☐
Bathroom 3	☐	☐	☐
Bonus / Game Room	☐	☐	☐

	Good	Average	Poor
Kitchen			
Cabinets	☐	☐	☐
Countertop	☐	☐	☐
Counter Space	☐	☐	☐
Flooring	☐	☐	☐
Oven / Stove	☐	☐	☐
Microwave	☐	☐	☐
Layout	☐	☐	☐
Light Fixtures	☐	☐	☐
Backsplash	☐	☐	☐
Pantry	☐	☐	☐
Appliances	☐	☐	☐
Island	☐	☐	☐

	Good	Average	Poor
Basement	☐	☐	☐
Garage	☐	☐	☐

COMMUNITY

	Good	Average	Poor
Immediate Neighborhood	☐	☐	☐
Close to Employment	☐	☐	☐
Close to Shopping	☐	☐	☐
Close to Transportation	☐	☐	☐
Close to Schools / Daycare	☐	☐	☐
Close to Places of Worship	☐	☐	☐
Near Recreational Facilities	☐	☐	☐
Close to Airport	☐	☐	☐
Near Police and Fire Department	☐	☐	☐

Address _____   Price _____

Bedrooms _____   Bathrooms _____   Sq.Ft. _____

Lot Size: _____   Year Built _____   School District _____

Annual Tax _____

EXTERIOR

	Good	Average	Poor
View/Yard/Landscaping	☐	☐	☐
Trees	☐	☐	☐
Lawn (Front)	☐	☐	☐
Lawn (Back)	☐	☐	☐
Fences (condition)	☐	☐	☐
Landscaping (condition)	☐	☐	☐
Irrigation / Sprinkler	☐	☐	☐
	☐	☐	☐
House Type	☐	☐	☐
Exterior Siding	☐	☐	☐
Deck / Patio / Porch	☐	☐	☐
Garage	☐	☐	☐
Window / Doors	☐	☐	☐
Roof / Gutters	☐	☐	☐
Fencing	☐	☐	☐

HOME SYSTEMS

	Good	Average	Poor
Electrical	☐	☐	☐
Air Conditioning / Fans	☐	☐	☐
Heating	☐	☐	☐
Security	☐	☐	☐
Plumbing	☐	☐	☐
Intercom	☐	☐	☐

FEATURES

	Good	Average	Poor
Home Warranty	☐	☐	☐
Energy Saving Features	☐	☐	☐

INTERIOR

	Good	Average	Poor
Walls / Trim / Ceilings	☐	☐	☐
Flooring	☐	☐	☐
Stairs	☐	☐	☐
Storage	☐	☐	☐
Living Room	☐	☐	☐
Family Room	☐	☐	☐
Dining Room	☐	☐	☐

	Good	Average	Poor
Master Bedroom	☐	☐	☐
Bedroom 2	☐	☐	☐
Bedroom 3	☐	☐	☐
Bedroom 4	☐	☐	☐
Master Bathroom	☐	☐	☐
Bathroom 2	☐	☐	☐
Bathroom 3	☐	☐	☐
Bonus / Game Room	☐	☐	☐

	Good	Average	Poor
Kitchen	☐	☐	☐
Cabinets	☐	☐	☐
Countertop	☐	☐	☐
Counter Space	☐	☐	☐
Flooring	☐	☐	☐
Oven / Stove	☐	☐	☐
Microwave	☐	☐	☐
Layout	☐	☐	☐
Light Fixtures	☐	☐	☐
Backsplash	☐	☐	☐
Pantry	☐	☐	☐
Appliances	☐	☐	☐
Island	☐	☐	☐

	Good	Average	Poor
Basement	☐	☐	☐
Garage	☐	☐	☐

COMMUNITY

	Good	Average	Poor
Immediate Neighborhood	☐	☐	☐
Close to Employment	☐	☐	☐
Close to Shopping	☐	☐	☐
Close to Transportation	☐	☐	☐
Close to Schools / Daycare	☐	☐	☐
Close to Places of Worship	☐	☐	☐
Near Recreational Facilities	☐	☐	☐
Close to Airport	☐	☐	☐
Near Police and Fire Department	☐	☐	☐

Address _____ Price _____

Bedrooms _____ Bathrooms _____ Sq.Ft. _____

Lot Size: _____ Year Built _____ School District _____

Annual Tax _____

EXTERIOR

	Good	Average	Poor
View/Yard/Landscaping	☐	☐	☐
Trees	☐	☐	☐
Lawn (Front)	☐	☐	☐
Lawn (Back)	☐	☐	☐
Fences (condition)	☐	☐	☐
Landscaping (condition)	☐	☐	☐
Irrigation / Sprinkler	☐	☐	☐
	☐	☐	☐
House Type	☐	☐	☐
Exterior Siding	☐	☐	☐
Deck / Patio / Porch	☐	☐	☐
Garage	☐	☐	☐
Window / Doors	☐	☐	☐
Roof / Gutters	☐	☐	☐
Fencing	☐	☐	☐

HOME SYSTEMS

	Good	Average	Poor
Electrical	☐	☐	☐
Air Conditioning / Fans	☐	☐	☐
Heating	☐	☐	☐
Security	☐	☐	☐
Plumbing	☐	☐	☐
Intercom	☐	☐	☐

FEATURES

	Good	Average	Poor
Home Warranty	☐	☐	☐
Energy Saving Features	☐	☐	☐

INTERIOR

	Good	Average	Poor
Walls / Trim / Ceilings	☐	☐	☐
Flooring	☐	☐	☐
Stairs	☐	☐	☐
Storage	☐	☐	☐
Living Room	☐	☐	☐
Family Room	☐	☐	☐
Dining Room	☐	☐	☐

	Good	Average	Poor
Master Bedroom	☐	☐	☐
Bedroom 2	☐	☐	☐
Bedroom 3	☐	☐	☐
Bedroom 4	☐	☐	☐
Master Bathroom	☐	☐	☐
Bathroom 2	☐	☐	☐
Bathroom 3	☐	☐	☐
Bonus / Game Room	☐	☐	☐

	Good	Average	Poor
Kitchen			
Cabinets	☐	☐	☐
Countertop	☐	☐	☐
Counter Space	☐	☐	☐
Flooring	☐	☐	☐
Oven / Stove	☐	☐	☐
Microwave	☐	☐	☐
Layout	☐	☐	☐
Light Fixtures	☐	☐	☐
Backsplash	☐	☐	☐
Pantry	☐	☐	☐
Appliances	☐	☐	☐
Island	☐	☐	☐

	Good	Average	Poor
Basement	☐	☐	☐
Garage	☐	☐	☐

COMMUNITY

	Good	Average	Poor
Immediate Neighborhood	☐	☐	☐
Close to Employment	☐	☐	☐
Close to Shopping	☐	☐	☐
Close to Transportation	☐	☐	☐
Close to Schools / Daycare	☐	☐	☐
Close to Places of Worship	☐	☐	☐
Near Recreational Facilities	☐	☐	☐
Close to Airport	☐	☐	☐
Near Police and Fire Department	☐	☐	☐

Address _____ Price _____

Bedrooms _____ Bathrooms _____ Sq.Ft. _____

Lot Size: _____ Year Built _____ School District _____

Annual Tax _____

EXTERIOR

	Good	Average	Poor
View/Yard/Landscaping	☐	☐	☐
Trees	☐	☐	☐
Lawn (Front)	☐	☐	☐
Lawn (Back)	☐	☐	☐
Fences (condition)	☐	☐	☐
Landscaping (condition)	☐	☐	☐
Irrigation / Sprinkler	☐	☐	☐
	☐	☐	☐
House Type	☐	☐	☐
Exterior Siding	☐	☐	☐
Deck / Patio / Porch	☐	☐	☐
Garage	☐	☐	☐
Window / Doors	☐	☐	☐
Roof / Gutters	☐	☐	☐
Fencing	☐	☐	☐

HOME SYSTEMS

	Good	Average	Poor
Electrical	☐	☐	☐
Air Conditioning / Fans	☐	☐	☐
Heating	☐	☐	☐
Security	☐	☐	☐
Plumbing	☐	☐	☐
Intercom	☐	☐	☐

FEATURES

	Good	Average	Poor
Home Warranty	☐	☐	☐
Energy Saving Features	☐	☐	☐

INTERIOR

	Good	Average	Poor
Walls / Trim / Ceilings	☐	☐	☐
Flooring	☐	☐	☐
Stairs	☐	☐	☐
Storage	☐	☐	☐
Living Room	☐	☐	☐
Family Room	☐	☐	☐
Dining Room	☐	☐	☐

	Good	Average	Poor
Master Bedroom	☐	☐	☐
Bedroom 2	☐	☐	☐
Bedroom 3	☐	☐	☐
Bedroom 4	☐	☐	☐
Master Bathroom	☐	☐	☐
Bathroom 2	☐	☐	☐
Bathroom 3	☐	☐	☐
Bonus / Game Room	☐	☐	☐

	Good	Average	Poor
Kitchen			
Cabinets	☐	☐	☐
Countertop	☐	☐	☐
Counter Space	☐	☐	☐
Flooring	☐	☐	☐
Oven / Stove	☐	☐	☐
Microwave	☐	☐	☐
Layout	☐	☐	☐
Light Fixtures	☐	☐	☐
Backsplash	☐	☐	☐
Pantry	☐	☐	☐
Appliances	☐	☐	☐
Island	☐	☐	☐

	Good	Average	Poor
Basement	☐	☐	☐
Garage	☐	☐	☐

COMMUNITY

	Good	Average	Poor
Immediate Neighborhood	☐	☐	☐
Close to Employment	☐	☐	☐
Close to Shopping	☐	☐	☐
Close to Transportation	☐	☐	☐
Close to Schools / Daycare	☐	☐	☐
Close to Places of Worship	☐	☐	☐
Near Recreational Facilities	☐	☐	☐
Close to Airport	☐	☐	☐
Near Police and Fire Department	☐	☐	☐

Address _____   Price _____

Bedrooms _____   Bathrooms _____   Sq.Ft. _____

Lot Size: _____   Year Built _____   School District _____

Annual Tax _____

EXTERIOR

	Good	Average	Poor
View/Yard/Landscaping	☐	☐	☐
Trees	☐	☐	☐
Lawn (Front)	☐	☐	☐
Lawn (Back)	☐	☐	☐
Fences (condition)	☐	☐	☐
Landscaping (condition)	☐	☐	☐
Irrigation / Sprinkler	☐	☐	☐
House Type	☐	☐	☐
Exterior Siding	☐	☐	☐
Deck / Patio / Porch	☐	☐	☐
Garage	☐	☐	☐
Window / Doors	☐	☐	☐
Roof / Gutters	☐	☐	☐
Fencing	☐	☐	☐

HOME SYSTEMS

	Good	Average	Poor
Electrical	☐	☐	☐
Air Conditioning / Fans	☐	☐	☐
Heating	☐	☐	☐
Security	☐	☐	☐
Plumbing	☐	☐	☐
Intercom	☐	☐	☐

FEATURES

	Good	Average	Poor
Home Warranty	☐	☐	☐
Energy Saving Features	☐	☐	☐

INTERIOR

	Good	Average	Poor
Walls / Trim / Ceilings	☐	☐	☐
Flooring	☐	☐	☐
Stairs	☐	☐	☐
Storage	☐	☐	☐
Living Room	☐	☐	☐
Family Room	☐	☐	☐
Dining Room	☐	☐	☐

	Good	Average	Poor
Master Bedroom	☐	☐	☐
Bedroom 2	☐	☐	☐
Bedroom 3	☐	☐	☐
Bedroom 4	☐	☐	☐
Master Bathroom	☐	☐	☐
Bathroom 2	☐	☐	☐
Bathroom 3	☐	☐	☐
Bonus / Game Room	☐	☐	☐

	Good	Average	Poor
Kitchen	☐	☐	☐
Cabinets	☐	☐	☐
Countertop	☐	☐	☐
Counter Space	☐	☐	☐
Flooring	☐	☐	☐
Oven / Stove	☐	☐	☐
Microwave	☐	☐	☐
Layout	☐	☐	☐
Light Fixtures	☐	☐	☐
Backsplash	☐	☐	☐
Pantry	☐	☐	☐
Appliances	☐	☐	☐
Island	☐	☐	☐

	Good	Average	Poor
Basement	☐	☐	☐
Garage	☐	☐	☐

COMMUNITY

	Good	Average	Poor
Immediate Neighborhood	☐	☐	☐
Close to Employment	☐	☐	☐
Close to Shopping	☐	☐	☐
Close to Transportation	☐	☐	☐
Close to Schools / Daycare	☐	☐	☐
Close to Places of Worship	☐	☐	☐
Near Recreational Facilities	☐	☐	☐
Close to Airport	☐	☐	☐
Near Police and Fire Department	☐	☐	☐

Address _____ Price _____

Bedrooms _____ Bathrooms _____ Sq.Ft. _____

Lot Size: _____ Year Built _____ School District _____

Annual Tax _____

EXTERIOR

	Good	Average	Poor
View/Yard/Landscaping	☐	☐	☐
Trees	☐	☐	☐
Lawn (Front)	☐	☐	☐
Lawn (Back)	☐	☐	☐
Fences (condition)	☐	☐	☐
Landscaping (condition)	☐	☐	☐
Irrigation / Sprinkler	☐	☐	☐
House Type	☐	☐	☐
Exterior Siding	☐	☐	☐
Deck / Patio / Porch	☐	☐	☐
Garage	☐	☐	☐
Window / Doors	☐	☐	☐
Roof / Gutters	☐	☐	☐
Fencing	☐	☐	☐

HOME SYSTEMS

	Good	Average	Poor
Electrical	☐	☐	☐
Air Conditioning / Fans	☐	☐	☐
Heating	☐	☐	☐
Security	☐	☐	☐
Plumbing	☐	☐	☐
Intercom	☐	☐	☐

FEATURES

	Good	Average	Poor
Home Warranty	☐	☐	☐
Energy Saving Features	☐	☐	☐

INTERIOR

	Good	Average	Poor
Walls / Trim / Ceilings	☐	☐	☐
Flooring	☐	☐	☐
Stairs	☐	☐	☐
Storage	☐	☐	☐
Living Room	☐	☐	☐
Family Room	☐	☐	☐
Dining Room	☐	☐	☐

	Good	Average	Poor
Master Bedroom	☐	☐	☐
Bedroom 2	☐	☐	☐
Bedroom 3	☐	☐	☐
Bedroom 4	☐	☐	☐
Master Bathroom	☐	☐	☐
Bathroom 2	☐	☐	☐
Bathroom 3	☐	☐	☐
Bonus / Game Room	☐	☐	☐

	Good	Average	Poor
Kitchen			
Cabinets	☐	☐	☐
Countertop	☐	☐	☐
Counter Space	☐	☐	☐
Flooring	☐	☐	☐
Oven / Stove	☐	☐	☐
Microwave	☐	☐	☐
Layout	☐	☐	☐
Light Fixtures	☐	☐	☐
Backsplash	☐	☐	☐
Pantry	☐	☐	☐
Appliances	☐	☐	☐
Island	☐	☐	☐

	Good	Average	Poor
Basement	☐	☐	☐
Garage	☐	☐	☐

COMMUNITY

	Good	Average	Poor
Immediate Neighborhood	☐	☐	☐
Close to Employment	☐	☐	☐
Close to Shopping	☐	☐	☐
Close to Transportation	☐	☐	☐
Close to Schools / Daycare	☐	☐	☐
Close to Places of Worship	☐	☐	☐
Near Recreational Facilities	☐	☐	☐
Close to Airport	☐	☐	☐
Near Police and Fire Department	☐	☐	☐

Address _____ Price _____

Bedrooms _____ Bathrooms _____ Sq.Ft. _____

Lot Size: _____ Year Built _____ School District _____

Annual Tax _____

EXTERIOR

	Good	Average	Poor
View/Yard/Landscaping	☐	☐	☐
Trees	☐	☐	☐
Lawn (Front)	☐	☐	☐
Lawn (Back)	☐	☐	☐
Fences (condition)	☐	☐	☐
Landscaping (condition)	☐	☐	☐
Irrigation / Sprinkler	☐	☐	☐
	☐	☐	☐
House Type	☐	☐	☐
Exterior Siding	☐	☐	☐
Deck / Patio / Porch	☐	☐	☐
Garage	☐	☐	☐
Window / Doors	☐	☐	☐
Roof / Gutters	☐	☐	☐
Fencing	☐	☐	☐

HOME SYSTEMS

	Good	Average	Poor
Electrical	☐	☐	☐
Air Conditioning / Fans	☐	☐	☐
Heating	☐	☐	☐
Security	☐	☐	☐
Plumbing	☐	☐	☐
Intercom	☐	☐	☐

FEATURES

	Good	Average	Poor
Home Warranty	☐	☐	☐
Energy Saving Features	☐	☐	☐

INTERIOR

	Good	Average	Poor
Walls / Trim / Ceilings	☐	☐	☐
Flooring	☐	☐	☐
Stairs	☐	☐	☐
Storage	☐	☐	☐
Living Room	☐	☐	☐
Family Room	☐	☐	☐
Dining Room	☐	☐	☐

	Good	Average	Poor
Master Bedroom	☐	☐	☐
Bedroom 2	☐	☐	☐
Bedroom 3	☐	☐	☐
Bedroom 4	☐	☐	☐
Master Bathroom	☐	☐	☐
Bathroom 2	☐	☐	☐
Bathroom 3	☐	☐	☐
Bonus / Game Room	☐	☐	☐

	Good	Average	Poor
Kitchen	☐	☐	☐
Cabinets	☐	☐	☐
Countertop	☐	☐	☐
Counter Space	☐	☐	☐
Flooring	☐	☐	☐
Oven / Stove	☐	☐	☐
Microwave	☐	☐	☐
Layout	☐	☐	☐
Light Fixtures	☐	☐	☐
Backsplash	☐	☐	☐
Pantry	☐	☐	☐
Appliances	☐	☐	☐
Island	☐	☐	☐

	Good	Average	Poor
Basement	☐	☐	☐
Garage	☐	☐	☐

COMMUNITY

	Good	Average	Poor
Immediate Neighborhood	☐	☐	☐
Close to Employment	☐	☐	☐
Close to Shopping	☐	☐	☐
Close to Transportation	☐	☐	☐
Close to Schools / Daycare	☐	☐	☐
Close to Places of Worship	☐	☐	☐
Near Recreational Facilities	☐	☐	☐
Close to Airport	☐	☐	☐
Near Police and Fire Department	☐	☐	☐

Address _____ Price _____

Bedrooms _____ Bathrooms _____ Sq.Ft. _____

Lot Size: _____ Year Built _____ School District _____

Annual Tax _____

EXTERIOR

	Good	Average	Poor
View/Yard/Landscaping	☐	☐	☐
Trees	☐	☐	☐
Lawn (Front)	☐	☐	☐
Lawn (Back)	☐	☐	☐
Fences (condition)	☐	☐	☐
Landscaping (condition)	☐	☐	☐
Irrigation / Sprinkler	☐	☐	☐
	☐	☐	☐
House Type	☐	☐	☐
Exterior Siding	☐	☐	☐
Deck / Patio / Porch	☐	☐	☐
Garage	☐	☐	☐
Window / Doors	☐	☐	☐
Roof / Gutters	☐	☐	☐
Fencing	☐	☐	☐

HOME SYSTEMS

	Good	Average	Poor
Electrical	☐	☐	☐
Air Conditioning / Fans	☐	☐	☐
Heating	☐	☐	☐
Security	☐	☐	☐
Plumbing	☐	☐	☐
Intercom	☐	☐	☐

FEATURES

	Good	Average	Poor
Home Warranty	☐	☐	☐
Energy Saving Features	☐	☐	☐

INTERIOR

	Good	Average	Poor
Walls / Trim / Ceilings	☐	☐	☐
Flooring	☐	☐	☐
Stairs	☐	☐	☐
Storage	☐	☐	☐
Living Room	☐	☐	☐
Family Room	☐	☐	☐
Dining Room	☐	☐	☐

	Good	Average	Poor
Master Bedroom	☐	☐	☐
Bedroom 2	☐	☐	☐
Bedroom 3	☐	☐	☐
Bedroom 4	☐	☐	☐
Master Bathroom	☐	☐	☐
Bathroom 2	☐	☐	☐
Bathroom 3	☐	☐	☐
Bonus / Game Room	☐	☐	☐

	Good	Average	Poor
Kitchen	☐	☐	☐
Cabinets	☐	☐	☐
Countertop	☐	☐	☐
Counter Space	☐	☐	☐
Flooring	☐	☐	☐
Oven / Stove	☐	☐	☐
Microwave	☐	☐	☐
Layout	☐	☐	☐
Light Fixtures	☐	☐	☐
Backsplash	☐	☐	☐
Pantry	☐	☐	☐
Appliances	☐	☐	☐
Island	☐	☐	☐

	Good	Average	Poor
Basement	☐	☐	☐
Garage	☐	☐	☐

COMMUNITY

	Good	Average	Poor
Immediate Neighborhood	☐	☐	☐
Close to Employment	☐	☐	☐
Close to Shopping	☐	☐	☐
Close to Transportation	☐	☐	☐
Close to Schools / Daycare	☐	☐	☐
Close to Places of Worship	☐	☐	☐
Near Recreational Facilities	☐	☐	☐
Close to Airport	☐	☐	☐
Near Police and Fire Department	☐	☐	☐

www.ingramcontent.com/pod-product-compliance
Lightning Source LLC
Chambersburg PA
CBHW070428220526
45466CB00004B/1590